Developing Distress Resolution Procedure

DEVELOPING DISTRESS RESOLUTION PROCEDURES FOR FINANCIAL INSTITUTIONS

By
Clas Wihlborg

SUERF – The European Money and Finance Forum
Vienna 2012

SUERF Study 2012/5

CIP

Developing Distress Resolution Procedures for Financial Institutions

Author: *Clas Wihlborg*

Keywords: Bank insolvency, Crisis resolution, Contagion

JEL Codes: G01, G18, G28

Vienna: SUERF (SUERF Studies: 2012/5) – August 2012

ISBN: 978-3-9021-0965-1

© 2012 SUERF, Vienna

TABLE OF CONTENTS

Developing Distress Resolution Procedures for Financial Institution

Clas Wihlborg[1]

Abstract

This paper focuses on the need for a *lex specialis* for resolution of insolvent banks and other financial institutions serving similar functions, and on requirements for making resolution procedures effective. After a review of the objectives of general insolvency law and the special characteristics of banks and the financial system, approaches to resolution procedures in a few 'model countries' are described. The issues that require attention in legislation for resolution procedures are identified as the contagion issue, the valuation issue, the predictability issue, the information issue, the coverage issue, the funding issue and the cross-border issue. Complementary reforms of the financial architecture that would enhance the effectiveness of legislation for resolution procedures are discussed as well[2].

1. Introduction

A common response of governments to signs of stress in the domestic banking system is to issue a blanket guarantee for banks' liabilities. For example, the Swedish government guaranteed all liabilities of domestic banks during the banking crisis in the early 1990s to prevent any kind of run on the banks and to allow them to have continued access to international markets for financing. Although the guarantee was legally abolished in 1995 the expectations that the government will behave the same way in another crisis naturally linger. Such expectations have been confirmed in the recent 2007-2009 crisis. Banks' creditors and, to some extent, shareholders have been provided with a safety-net across Europe.

Only in the US have bank failures been allowed to result in losses for large groups of creditors. Even there, large banks and other financial institutions (with the exception of Lehman Brothers) were protected and bailed out. The non-bailout of Lehman has been viewed as the cause of a deepening of the crisis in September 2008. Although this view of the consequences of the Lehman failure is controversial, it has reinforced the fear of allowing large financial institutions to fail.

Another consequence of the recent crisis is that public sentiment has turned strongly against the use of tax-payer money to bail out financial institutions in

---

[1]   Chapman University, Orange, CA. A first draft of this paper was written for the Swedish Government Audit Office (Riksrevisionen) in October 2010.
[2]   I am grateful to James B. Thomson for comments and corrections on an earlier version.

the US, in particular, but public opinion in many European countries seems to have moved in the same direction. There is now political pressure in many countries to develop legal and regulatory institutions that will make large scale bailouts unnecessary or less costly to tax payers in the future. The European Commission has proposed a tax on banks with the objective of building up funds to cope with a future crisis. Sweden has enacted such a tax and the National Debt Office has been appointed to act as Resolution Authority with responsibility for putting the funds to use as part its management of the resolution process for banks in distress. The Dodd-Frank financial reform bill in the US proposes the creation of an 'Orderly Dissolution Fund' paid for by financial companies to be used for resolution of distressed financial institutions.

The existence of a fund for dealing with the costs of a crisis can strengthen the expectations that banks will be bailed out again in a crisis unless there are effective and credible procedures for allowing banks to fail with consequences for uninsured creditors. The longer term adverse effect of not allowing large financial institutions to fail is that creditors worry less about their solvency and, as a result, creditors monitor them less intensively. Thereby, the protected financial institutions gain a competitive advantage through lower costs of funds. This implicit subsidization leads to further concentration in the financial industry and implicit protection of an increasing share of the financial industry. It is well-known and empirically well documented that financial institutions, wherein creditors are largely protected, have incentives to take excessive risk since part of the downside is carried by tax payers and deposit insurance funds.

The incentives to take excessive risk associated with explicit and implicit protection of banks' creditors are not typically revealed as deliberate opportunistic behavior of bank managers. Risk-taking is the result of an artificially low cost of debt relative to the cost of equity and insensitivity of the cost of debt to increased risk. Banks facing competition seek to minimize the cost of capital and, at a given cost of funds; banks will seek to maximize the return on capital. With weak monitoring from creditors and a low penalty for risk-taking, the industry standards for proper risk management and risk awareness declines. As a result, banks tend to neglect that relatively high return assets often are associated with relatively high risk without being penalized. Liquidity risk may similarly become excessive and reveal itself in increased short term funding of long term commitments.

The Basel Committee on Banking Supervision acknowledges that in a market economy, failures are part of risk-taking and that a prompt and orderly liquidation of financial institutions that are no longer able to meet supervisory requirements is a necessary part of an efficient financial system. Forbearance often leads to worsening problems and higher resolution costs. On the other hand, the Committee explicitly states that "in some cases the best interests of depositors may be served by some form of restructuring, possibly takeover by a stronger institution or injection of new capital or shareholder." Prior to the crisis the Committee's, as well as the European Commission's, focus was on shareholders having to face responsibility for losses. However, it is the protection of creditors that reduces the cost of debt financing. Creditors do not penalize risk-taking sufficiently and they do not have strong incentives to monitor banks' behavior. Under limited liability shareholders have incentives to 'gamble for survival' when the equity capital at stake falls in value.

The focus on shareholders' responsibility for losses may explain why the Basel Committee before the crisis did not pay much attention to the development of explicit procedures for bank distress resolution including procedures for allocating losses to banks' creditors. Even procedures for 'structured early intervention' along the lines of the US rules for Prompt Corrective Action (PCA) were neglected or deemed 'too Anglo-Saxon' on the European Continent.

Another reason why formal insolvency procedures for financial institutions have been neglected may be a common belief that banking crises are often caused by systemic shocks that tend to put a large part of the banking system in distress at one time. Subjecting a large part of the system to insolvency procedures at one time seems unimaginable and, therefore, protecting the system by taking over its losses is viewed as the only acceptable alternative. A consequence of this view is that insolvency procedures become almost superfluous as instruments of crisis management. The argument misses the point that even a large macroeconomic shock need not threaten the whole financial systems if financial institutions are not excessively fragile. The fragility of the whole system is partly caused by distorted risk-taking incentives associated with lack of market discipline on risk-taking. Thus, if effective insolvency procedures can contribute to market discipline, the likelihood of facing a crisis wherein the whole system is facing insolvency is reduced. In other words, the insolvency procedures should improve the ability of the system as a whole to handle a large macroeconomic shock without system wide insolvencies.

Several economists have discussed the potential contribution of bank insolvency law in enhancing market discipline in Europe, where specific bank crisis resolution procedures had not been implemented before the crisis[3]. The European Shadow Financial Regulatory Committee (1998) expressed the objective of a special insolvency law for banks in the following way: "The implementation of insolvency law for banks… should achieve an acceptable, low risk of runs and low risk of contagion while inefficient owners and managers exit. The contractual predict-

---

[3]   See Angkinand and Wihlborg (2006), Eisenbeis and Kaufman (2007, 2008), Goldberg, Sweeney and Wihlborg (2005), Huertas (2007), Hupkes (2003), Krimminger (2005), Lastra and Wihlborg (2007), Llewellyn and Mayes (2003), Schiffman (1999).

ability of claims and the predictability of bankruptcy and PCA (Prompt Corrective Action)-costs should provide efficient ex ante incentives. By achieving these objectives the government's and the regulator's fear of a system crash should be alleviated. Thereby, non-insurance of groups of creditors and shareholders would be credible."

In a similar vein, The Economist wrote more recently[4] that "What is needed is a way of pushing losses onto creditors without sparking a run that endangers the whole system." The editorial continues to note that "The alternative (to break up large banks into banks small enough to fail) is to find a way to allow a controlled default of part of banks' balance sheets. That will require the rejigging of their liabilities to include new forms of debt, as well as the creation of resolution authorities with enough power to impose losses on some creditors, but not so much that they terrify counterparties into running."

Llewellyn (2010) has suggested that a fourth pillar should be added to the three pillars of the Basel Capital Accord. This fourth pillar should focus on resolution arrangements including structured early intervention and rules for activation of the procedures with the objective of reducing costs of bank failures.

Procedures for structured early intervention and allocation of losses to creditors in case of insolvency need to be designed with the special characteristics of financial firms in mind in the sense that they minimize the risk of contagion among financial institutions. Without predictable rules for the allocation of losses, resolution will be delayed and, in the meantime, management and shareholders of distressed firms are likely to try to avoid the realization of losses in various ways. Expectations of government intervention may delay the realization of losses further.

During the recent crisis the G-20 and others have suggested that large financial institutions should plan for their own unwinding while in good health by means of Recovery and Resolution Plans (Living Wills). Such plans cannot substitute for formal procedures but the information required in Living Wills can be made part of 'structured early intervention' as suggested by, for example, Avgouleas *et al.* (2010) and Llewellyn (2010). We return to this issue below.

In the following, the role of insolvency procedures and criteria for efficiency of insolvency procedures for non-financial corporations are reviewed in Section 2. The traditional view of banks' specialness and the argument for special bank insolvency law is discussed in Section 3. In Section 4 the specialness of banks relative to other financial institutions is questioned based on experiences of systemic risk in the recent financial crisis. The argument that the closure of large

---

[4]   Editorial on January 30, 2010.

insolvent banks or a large part of the banking system in a crisis is not feasible is discussed in Section 5. Existing procedures for dealing with and resolving distress and insolvency of banks are reviewed in Section 6 with a focus on the US, New Zealand, the UK and Denmark as 'model countries'. This review leads to the identification of key issues that must be addressed in the design of insolvency procedures and distress resolution more broadly. The following issues are discussed in Section 7:

a.   the contagion issue;
b.   the valuation issue;
c.   the predictability issue;
d.   the information issue;
e.   the coverage issue;
d.   the funding issue;
g.   the cross-border issue.

Even the best insolvency law cannot deal with all problems associated with excessive risk-taking and systemic risk. The need for complementary reform is discussed in Section 8. Concluding remarks and notes on ongoing work in international organizations follow in Section 9.

2.   THE ROLE AND EFFICIENCY OF CORPORATE INSOLVENCY LAW

Efficient corporate insolvency procedures allow appropriate restructuring, debt-reduction, management change, liquidity infusion or other actions to take place. Debt reduction or forgiveness allows a person or a firm to 'start over without the burden of old debt'. The difficulty of designing efficient insolvency procedures is to a large extent caused by information problems with respect to the cause of distress and asset values. Collateralized loans and priority rules discourage 'runs' on the available resources of a distressed firm. A run can force a firm into bankruptcy prematurely. In banking this 'run problem' is particularly acute. Another issue discussed below is that efficient insolvency procedures at the time insolvency occurs need not be efficient *ex ante* when incentives for taking on debt and risk must be considered.

In countries with explicit corporate restructuring law such as Chapter 11 in the US, an independent body with enforcement powers, such as a court, is required to determine the value of the firm and the value-maximizing course of action. Contracts are abrogated when firms enter restructuring proceedings. Therefore, the predictability of the outcome for various stakeholders is low and the outcome is generally more favorable to the shareholders and management than the outcomes in countries with a more creditor-and liquidation oriented approach to insolvency[5]. The predictability of formal insolvency procedures is also influenced by arbitrariness of court procedures, corruption of judges, and political influences on the procedures. Clearly, the nature of the insolvency procedures and their predictability affect the process of loss allocation, its speed, and the ability of different stakeholders to influence the allocation of losses.

According to Schiffman[6], corporate insolvency laws should seek to fulfill two principal objectives: fair and predictable treatment of creditors and maximization of assets of the debtor in the interests of creditors.

Forgiveness of debt allows a person or a firm to start over without being burdened by previous mistakes but expected forgiveness may provide incentives to borrow in excess of what is *ex ante* efficient. A 'time consistency problem' exists when the efficient action against an insolvent firm or individual at the time of the insolvency event is different from the efficient procedures to be incorporated in persons' and firms' borrowing and project decisions. The 'first best' approach to resolve the insolvency at the time of the event may include forgiveness of debt but, if forgiveness is expected, the likelihood of insolvency could increase as a result of incentives to borrow and take risk. In this case, lenders are likely to reduce the supply of credit in this situation but with imperfect information about the honesty of the borrower and the risk he or she is taking. A second best solution at the time of insolvency may include a penalty on the person becoming insolvent in order to create superior *ex ante* incentives to reduce the demand for credit.

3. THE SPECIAL CHARACTERISTICS OF BANKS. THE NEED FOR LEX SPECIALIS

In banking there are potential externalities associated with insolvency which make the time consistency issue particularly relevant. It is widely accepted that one bank's failure can lead to a 'domino effect' threatening the banking system. If so, the first best response to a bank's insolvency may be to bail out the bank or in other ways protect its creditors. Expecting a bail-out the bank's shareholders have an incentive to leverage the bank excessively. Protection of creditors in the case of insolvency may prevent 'domino effects' but, if the protection is expected, the supply of credit to the bank becomes excessive and there is no incentive for creditors to monitor the bank's risk-taking. Limited liability of shareholders has the same effect on incentives. In general, the bank will find it optimal to accept a relatively high probability of insolvency.

---

[5]   See Wihlborg, Gangopadhyay and Hussain (2001).
[6]   See H. Schiffman (1999), pp. 89-90.

As for persons and firms, an ex ante rule for loss sharing in case of insolvency could reduce the demand for, as well as the supply of, borrowed funds to the bank. Although the rule would be second best at the time of insolvency, it could provide more efficient incentives for risk-taking in the banking system.

The time consistent rule would occur when the expected degree of bail-out and creditor protection reflects the actual bail out and creditor protection policy. There are multiple time consistent rules and policies but the efficient one would induce risk-taking in accordance with households' preferences for risk. For a rule to be time-consistent it must be made credible by the loss allocation at the time of insolvency. Since insolvency is not an everyday event the credibility may have to be supported by an institutional framework providing commitment to the rule.

Although the roles of insolvency procedures for banks in some ways are the same as for non-financial corporations, the objectives of the procedures differ in important ways. These differences are explained by the special characteristics of banks and other financial firms as mentioned above and discussed in more detail below. Speed of action in distress resolution is of the essence. Conventional liquidation and restructuring procedures are too time-consuming to be applied to banks without modification.

For the reasons mentioned, corporate bankruptcy-and restructuring laws are not often applied in cases when banks fall under the jurisdiction of these laws. Before the subprime crisis few countries had special insolvency law for banks and other financial firms, however[7]. The main exception was the USA where bank-specific insolvency procedures were implemented in 1991 through the enactment of FDICIA (Federal Deposit Insurance Corporation Improvement Act). A bank reaching a capital ratio of two percent is put under the receivership of the FDIC. The specific rules for resolving the distressed bank under the FDICIA are described in Section 6 below. Several hundred small and medium-sized banks were closed during the years 2008-2010. The procedures have so far not been tested on a large bank, however.

It seems appropriate that the insuring authority like the FDIC takes the coordinating role that large, senior creditors often have in non-bank re-structuring. However, in many countries the insuring authority may be the government and, even if there is a specific authority, there are in most countries neither pre-established procedures for settling claims against non-insured creditors, nor the expertise in the authority to manage the insolvency.

---

[7] Other countries with explicit procedures for bank insolvencies before the crisis were New Zealand, Brazil, Canada and Italy. After the crisis the number of countries with explicit law with respect to bank insolvencies has been growing and new laws are considered and debated in many countries. Some examples will be discussed below.

In banking, the definition of insolvency (the trigger point for an insolvency pro-
ceeding) is sometimes a matter or controversy. There are two traditional definitions of insolvency in commercial bankruptcy laws: failure to pay obligations as
they fall due (equitable insolvency), and liabilities exceed assets (balance sheet
insolvency)[8]. In banking the line of demarcation between illiquidity (lack of liquid
funds) and insolvency is not always clear. An economically insolvent bank is not
always declared legally insolvent by the responsible authorities and may be
offered financial assistance instead.

The pre-insolvency phase is of great importance in banking because of the difficulty of evaluating when the net worth of a bank is zero in market terms. In recent
years PCA (prompt corrective action) rules, including SEIR (structured early
intervention rules for action at trigger points while there is equity capital left)
have been advocated. In the USA, legally binding PCA rules exist since the enactment of FDICIA in 1991. This Act makes the structured early intervention legally
binding in order to enhance credibility and predictability of actions against distressed banks.

An important function of structured early intervention rules is to allow intervention before insolvency occurs in order to rehabilitate or restructure a distressed
bank. Laws with respect to bank rehabilitation, reorganization or restructuring
vary widely from country to country. A takeover or a merger generally preserves
the going-concern value of an institution, as the acquirer succeeds both to a
depositor base and to a base of loan customers. As opposed to a straight liquidation, a merger eliminates the danger that vital banking services in a community
will be disrupted. Sometimes, failed banks may be placed under special administration in the form of bridge banks or other arrangements. These are often meant
to be temporary solutions in order to take over the operations of the failed bank
and preserve its going-concern value while the government fiduciary seeks a more
permanent solution to the problems or until an acquirer is found. We return to
these procedures below.

4.   NEW VIEWS OF SYSTEMIC RISK. ARE BANKS REALLY
SPECIAL?

The traditional arguments for government regulation of industries are to con-
strain monopoly power and the existence of externalities. In the financial sector
the externality most often emphasized is that the failure of a bank can threaten
the payment system as a consequence of contagion of one bank's failure through
the banking system. The contagion could occur through runs on solvent banks

---

[8]   See Schiffmann (1999), pp. 96-97.

because they are opaque and through inter-bank claims arising within payment and settlement systems.

In the traditional view banks were special as a result of their participation in payment systems and as suppliers of liquidity. These roles of banks imply that very short term liabilities provide most of their funding while longer term, illiquid loans dominate on the assets side.

The interconnectedness of banks implies that there is a substantial difference between the failure of a bank and the failure of, for example, a car manufacturer. One car manufacturer's failure improves the profitability of others. One bank's failure can lead to losses for other banks with claims on the failing bank.

It can be debated whether the contagion effect in banking is a true externality since the individual bank evaluating the risk of lending to another bank should take into account the probability that systemic problems can arise as one factor in the lending and pricing decision. Whether we want to call the contagion effect an externality or not, the fact remains that the distress of one large bank or several small banks can have system-wide consequences and each bank may not take these potential consequences fully into account in their risk and liquidity management.

The sub-prime financial crisis has led to increased awareness that the failure of non-bank financial institutions can create contagion effects as well. Thus, in addition to bank contagion mentioned above, there are channels of contagion we can call price contagion and liquidity contagion.

Price contagion occurs through securities markets when a large financial institution must sell assets quickly resulting in a decline in asset values throughout the financial system. This type of contagion has increased in importance as a result of increased reliance on mark-to-market valuation and higher capital requirements.

Liquidity contagion refers to lack of liquidity in securities markets with the consequence that financial institutions wanting to or having to sell securities have difficulties finding buyers at prices corresponding to conventional economic values. The lack of liquidity may arise as a result of uncertainty about the solvency of financial institutions. Thus, the source of this type of contagion can be similar to the bank run problem caused by market participants' inability to identify the insolvent banks. If there is fear of a liquidity squeeze, financial institutions may also hoard liquidity out of fear that they may not be able to sell when needed. In this case, one financial institution may look liquid on the balance sheet but this liquidity could contribute to lack of liquidity in securities markets.

These types of contagion have in common that they affect non-bank financial institutions as well as traditional banks, and that they are likely to have repercussions on the real economy when the financial institutions reduce the supply of credit in order to retain or build up capital or retain or build up liquidity. The contagion effects are particularly severe for financial institutions with substantial mismatch of maturities of assets and liabilities. As the crisis has demonstrated non-banks often financed the purchase of long term securities in the markets for short term securities such as commercial papers. Cohen (2008) reports that Bear Stearns funded much lending activity through overnight borrowing.

Price and liquidity contagion are likely to reinforce each other since the market value of securities can drop dramatically when buyers require a substantial liquidity premium and, therefore, bid below the traditional economic value. Mark-to-market valuation clearly plays an important role in the process.

Brunnermeier *et al.* (2009) discuss the process of contagion through securities markets. They point out two externalities in a market-based financial system:
1.   fire sale externalities;
2.   interconnectedness externalities.

The fire sale externality implies that financial institutions do not take into account the price impact on other institutions of their sales in a possible future liquidity crunch. The interconnectedness externality refers to the case when a financial institution does not consider consequences of their actions on connected institutions that may suffer losses as a result of its actions.

To analyze these externalities further Brunnermeier *et al.* elaborate on alternative models of contagion. The traditional 'domino model' refers to the traditional bank contagion model. One bank's insolvency implies a loss for another bank and if this loss is big enough it will default with consequences for a third bank and so on. Most studies of this domino effect conclude that its impact on contagion is small.

An additional consideration from a systemic point of view is that lack of market liquidity and price effects can amplify the systemic effects of losses incurred by one bank. One bank suffering losses draws down its balance sheet including claims on another bank. This second bank must find a new source of funding. Without access to another source it must sell assets and thereby depress prices.

Brunnermeier *et al.* describe the potentially serious systemic 'loss spiral' for financial institutions caused by price effects in securities markets[9]. To start the downward spiral they consider a fall in the price of a security held by hedge funds and banks. The net worth of the financial institution falls more than the price. To restore the equity cushion the institution sells assets to repay debt. The asset price falls further impacting on the equity cushion of other financial insti-

---

9   Brunnermeier *et al.* (2009) base their descriptions of loss spirals on M. Brunnermeier and L. Pedersen, "Market Liquidity and Funding Liquidity", *Review of Financial Studies* 2009.

tutions. Mark-to-market valuation plays an important role in the process that works in reverse as well.

The loss spiral can be amplified further by a 'margin/haircut spiral' in leveraged financial institutions. Margins and haircuts determine the maximum leverage a financial institution can choose. An increase in margins forces the financial institution to sell assets to de-leverage. Asset prices fall and financial institutions must sell more assets to de-leverage further and so on. If many market participants find themselves in a similar situation there are no buyers and liquidity disappears with the result that the price drops become more accentuated.

Adrian and Shin (2007) present evidence of this spiral showing that there is a strong positive correlation between change in leverage and change in assets. The percent change in asset (change in log assets) is on the average equal to the percent change in leverage (change in log assets-change in log equity). This observation implies that adjustment in leverage takes place mostly through asset expansion and contraction and not through equity adjustment. This pattern is consistent with the margin/haircut spiral reinforcing the asset price spiral. These spirals have the effect of causing pro-cyclicality in the reaction of financial institutions to changes in asset prices over the cycle.

The expanded view of contagion and systemic risk summarized above has strong implications for the regulation and supervision of the financial sector. One is that contagion and, thereby, systemic effects of financial institution's distress is not confined to traditional banking in the modern financial system. A maturity mismatch between assets and liabilities of banks as well as non-bank financial institutions makes the financial system vulnerable to liquidity shocks.

Another implication is that mark-to-market accounting contributes to 'price contagion' and the pro-cyclicality of financial activity. It does not necessarily follow, however, that mark-to-market accounting should be abandoned. Instead, capital adequacy regulation with its rigid minimum capital ratio may have to be reconsidered. Transparency with respect to valuation of assets is important because it contributes to transparency with respect to solvency and, thereby, to a lower likelihood of that a financial institution will face liquidity problems.

These implications of the modern analysis of contagion have direct relevance for the regulatory framework for financial institutions including procedures for dealing with financial institutions in distress. The following observations can be made with respect to the legal and regulatory framework for financial institutions:

(i) special insolvency law may have to cover non-bank financial institutions as well as banks;

(ii) flexibility in the required capital ratio can reduce the need for fire sales of assets. 'Structured early intervention' prior to insolvency along the lines of

Prompt Corrective Action procedures is one way of achieving flexibility while reducing the probability that a financial institution will reach the default point;

(iii) principles for valuation of assets should be transparent and clear since they affect points of intervention and insolvency;

(iv) insolvency procedures need to be specified with one objective being to minimize the asset price effects and market liquidity effects of one institution's default;

(v) it must be recognized that the procedures for dealing with a financial institution in distress affect the incentives for risk-taking and liquidity planning (including mismatch of maturities) prior to insolvency;

(vi) valuation principles affect these incentives as well. For example, mark-to-market accounting is associated with greater risk of insolvency as well as liquidity problems at a given capital ratio and maturity mismatch. On the other hand, the greater variability of market prices can provide incentives to raise capital ratios and improve liquidity planning.

5. CAN THE MARKET HANDLE THE INSOLVENCY OF A LARGE FINANCIAL INSTITUTION?

Many observers of the financial crisis have argued that it was made unnecessarily severe by Lehman Brothers default on September 15, 2008. The most common description of events is that banks' short term cost of funding shot up and liquidity in short term securities markets dried up. Most economists and policy makers use these observations from the time of Lehman Brothers' default as evidence that large financial institutions must not be allowed to fail because, if they default, the systemic consequences can cause a disastrous credit crunch and, therefore, depression.

A smaller group of economists dispute both the evidence of the market's reaction to Lehman's default and the explanations for the credit crunch and decline in economic activity that followed. In particular, Cochrane and Zingales in an article in Wall Street Journal on the anniversary of Lehman's default showed evidence that the bank-credit default swap spread (the cost of buying insurance against default) on September 22, 2008 one week after the default was down on the same level as on September 12 a few days before the default. Thus, it seems that the markets absorbed Lehman Brothers' default within a week. On September 25 the spread was up again, however. What happened between September 22 and September 25 that could raise the spreads again?

Cochrane and Zingales note that on September 23 and 24 the Chairman of the Federal Reserve Board, Ben Bernanke, and the Treasury Secretary, Henry Paulson, gave speeches to congress requesting $700 billion for the Troubled Asset Relief Program (TARP). The LIBOR-OIS spread capturing the riskiness of short term interbank lending shot up 60 points from September 23 to September 25 while it rose only 18 points the day of Lehman's collapse. How can an announcement of massive aid to financial institutions lead to an increase in risk-spreads and a collapse of liquidity in short term markets?

The Cochrane-Zingales story is that the speeches by Bernanke and Paulson amounted to saying "The financial system is about to collapse. We can't tell you why. We need $700 billion. We can't tell you what we are going to do with it."

Actually, the Fed and the Treasury had felt for some time that they may need authority to carry out bail-outs but in Cochrane-Zingales interpretation the public saw a government in panic and banks in worse trouble than previously thought.

The more common interpretation of Lehman as the cause of the deepening crisis leads to the policy implication that the government must have bail-out power and ability to avert serious systemic consequences of the default of large financial institutions. The Cochrane-Zingales interpretation has the implication that markets can adjust reasonably quickly to the default of one institution, even one as large as Lehman Brothers. Most of the Lehman's operations were up and running with new owners within a few days and losses were to a large extent allocated to various creditors. There were problems though when, for example, repos were stuck in a UK bankruptcy court.

The Lehman bankruptcy was carried out under bankruptcy laws intended for corporations in the UK as well as the US[10]. It is not surprising that there were some problems. Nevertheless, there was no great wave of contagion to creditors of Lehman.

The main implication of Cochrane and Zingales' analysis is that systemic liquidity problems can arise when financial institution are induced to hoard available liquidity out of fear that funding in the market may not be available when needed and as a result of uncertainty about the soundness of each financial institutions trying to borrow funds in the market. The consequences of these liquidity problems are likely to be more severe the longer the time the 'clean-up' of the system is expected to take.

In another paper Cochrane (2009) draws the conclusion that "once everyone expects a bail out, it (the government) has to bail out or chaos results." The expectation of bail out of large institutions creates a competitive advantage for

---

[10] In most cases bankruptcies under Chapter 11 in the US are time consuming and characterized by long negotiations about loss allocation.

large, interconnected and opaque institutions. If so, there are incentives to organize financial activities in such financial institutions. Externalities creating systemic risk are thereby created by the fear of systemic risk.

Cochrane (2009) does not draw the conclusion that regulation is unnecessary. Regulation must deal with the problem that explicit insurance of some depositors creates incentives to use deposited funds for risky activities but regulation and tax systems should not encourage the creation of obscure and fragile institutions. One example is the Special Investment Vehicles that invested in mortgage backed securities funded by short term commercial papers explicitly or implicitly guaranteed by a bank.

Funding for financial institutions beyond the necessary explicit insurance must be explicitly risky for investors. Investors facing default risk of financial institutions would penalize the overly opaque and interconnected financial institution since it would be subject to greater risk including the risk of contagion from others market participants. This view implies that the externalities discussed above can be reduced in a financial system where opaqueness and interconnectedness are penalized by creditors of financial institutions.

The procedures for dealing with the large financial institution are not addressed in the mentioned papers. However, Cochrane notes that the creation of a resolution authority does not in itself reduce the likelihood of bail-outs but that the likelihood may actually increase if the resolution authority is given a large amount of arbitrary power with few legal constraints. Thus, predictability of rules for allocation of losses is an essential part of insolvency procedures if bail-out incentives are to be reduced.

A more detailed view of the market's ability to deal with a large financial conglomerate in distress is given by Huertas (2007). He argues that the financial infrastructure has become sufficiently robust to handle even the largest financial institution's default as a result of increased robustness of payments, clearing and settlement systems. On these grounds Huertas proposes that in a large crisis affecting most of the financial system the public authority should consider the use of liquidity creating powers to prevent the second large failure but not the first.

Huertas points to several robustness-enhancing financial developments in recent decades and to potential innovations that would contribute further to robustness. First, capital markets can provide funds even to very large firms if investors can be convinced that a distressed firm has a viable strategy for correcting past errors. Funding can be obtained in the form of common equity, mezzanine financing (preferred stock and subordinated debt), securitization and structured finance in various forms. The sale of a part of the conglomerate is another source. Subordinated debt can be made convertible into equity at a critical level of distress.

Flannery (2005) and Östrup (2008) have suggested mandatory convertible debt (CoCos) as a part of the regulatory capital[11].

Capital markets can also provide protection in advance of distress by means of financial instruments that pay out contingent on an event and/or level of equity. Contingent capital is offered by insurance companies. Catastrophe bonds are a form of derivative that pays out if losses exceed a certain trigger coupled with a fund invested in low risk securities to eliminate counterparty risk.

Another factor pointed out by Huertas is the increased robustness of payment systems as a result of real-time gross settlement systems and multilateral netting. According to the Lamfalussy principles[12] a multilateral netting system "should, at a minimum, be capable of ensuring the timely completion of daily settlements in the event of an inability to settle by the largest single settlement obligation." Furthermore, the system should have a well-founded legal basis under all relevant jurisdictions." Essentially, operations of payment and settlement systems should be insulated from the bankruptcy of operations. Bankruptcy codes are not consistent with this principle in some jurisdictions but in the EU payment and settlement systems have been 'carved out' from insolvency law (EU Directive on Settlement Finality in Payment and Securities Settlement systems (1998/26 OJ L. 166, 11/06/1088).

The so called Herstatt risk in foreign exchange markets[13] has also been reduced substantially through the introduction of the CLS bank in 2002. This bank is owned by a group of large banks and its purpose is to settle foreign exchange transactions on a continuous basis. The bank matches foreign exchange transactions, provides for multilateral netting and arranges for settlement of net obligations. Participating banks post collateral with the CLS Bank.

The third robustness factor pointed out by Huertas is the implementation of standards for documentation of derivatives contracts. The standards have been negotiated through the ISDA (International Swap Dealers Association). The documentation allows for bilateral close-out netting within and between countries. Remaining exposures are often collateralized[14].

Turning finally to securities markets, robustness has improved through improvements in payment, clearing and settlements systems. In addition, the Group of Thirty (2003:2), building on earlier recommendations to reduce the risk in clearing and settlement systems made recommendations with the objective to develop an efficient and safe global network for securities market trading. In particular

---

[11]   In 2005 there was about USD 25 billion in mandatory convertible bank debt outstanding according to Huertas. Credit Suisse Group issued CHF 1 billion in 2002.
[12]   Committee on Payment and Settlement Systems (1997).
[13]   Herstatt risk occurs when banks settle one leg of a foreign exchange transaction in advance of the other.
[14]   In 2005 55 percent of OTC derivatives exposures was supported by collateral according to Huertas (2007).

'automation and acceleration of trade matching and confirmation' by means of common technical and communication standards have been emphasized. The greatest progress in this respect has been made in the EU[15]. Furthermore, the interval between trade date and settlement data has been shortened to three to four days and a Central Counterparty (CCP) has been created. The CCP is the buyer for every seller and the seller to every buyer. The CCP takes the counterparty risk. To reduce the risk of failure of the CCP it limits its exposure to each participant and requires collateral for remaining exposures.

The mentioned measures to increase the robustness of the financial system has contributed to making the so called domino effect a minor source of contagion among traditional banks as well as among other financial institutions including conglomerates. Contagion through price and liquidity effects have not been eliminated, however, as demonstrated by the recent financial crisis. Since these effects are closely associated with macroeconomic economic developments, Huertas (2007) emphasizes the provision of liquidity of the central bank as a key instrument to dampen the contagion and mitigate its effects. This route has also been followed by central banks in the current crisis.

Brunnermeier *et al.* (2009) referred to in the previous section emphasize these sources of contagion as macro-prudential concerns. They also emphasize that inability to distinguish between solvency and liquidity problems contributes to contagion. Cochrane's view is that the vulnerability to contagion is very much a result of explicit and implicit protection of creditors, in particular, and the impact of this protection on incentives to create large opaque institutions that become vulnerable to liquidity shocks.

Huerta's relatively optimistic view of the market's ability to manage the insolvency of a large bank (or a large part of the banking system) is based on the presumption that market participants are able to distinguish between banks with and without viable strategies for the future. Thus, a degree of transparency of operations and bank exposures is required. This transparency seems to have been lacking during the crisis years. As a result the liquidity support during the crisis had to be much larger than required in a less opaque financial system.

The transparency, or lack thereof, of risk exposures cannot be taken as given in an analysis of reforms of the financial system and insolvency procedures, in particular. Transparency depends on incentives of financial institutions to disclose and signal relevant information about their health. If insolvency law contributes to making losses for creditors a real possibility, banks in good health have a strong incentive to disclose and signal relevant information. Thereby, contagion to these banks is less likely. On the other hand, if banks' creditors expect bail-

---

[15]   Group of Thirty (2005, pp. 3-4 and 16-18).

outs, transparency becomes less important to the creditors. Incentives of bank managers of healthy banks to provide transparency are also reduced if promises of aid to ailing banks have been made. Thus, the strength of contagion is likely to be reduced if effective insolvency procedures are in place.

The emphasis on price and liquidity effects as sources of contagion implies also that it is not primarily the size of a financial institution in distress that should concern the policy-makers. Instead the magnitude of the shock hitting the financial system affects asset prices and the incentives for fire sales. It matters less whether one large or 10 smaller financial institutions are affected in a similar way by a shock to the financial system. Given the size of the shock it is transparency of risk exposures or lack thereof that determines whether market participants are able to identify which financial institutions are most affected by a shock. The less transparency the greater is the danger of liquidity contagion.

6.   APPROACHES TO BANK INSOLVENCY

In this section the main elements of resolution procedures for financial institutions are described with a focus on the US, New Zealand and the UK. The insolvency regimes in these countries are often viewed as 'models' for other countries. Insolvency regimes in Denmark and a few other countries and current efforts to develop an EU regime are discussed briefly as well.

6.1.   The US approach[16]

US law with respect to insolvency prior to and during the crisis separated the treatment of banks from the treatment of non-financial and other corporations. Insolvency procedures for banks were specified in the FDICIA (Federal Deposit Insurance Improvement Act of 1991)[17]. The main elements of the FDICIA remain in effect after the crisis, although some of the aspects of the Dodd-Frank bill will have consequences for the future handling of distress financial institutions. We return to Dodd-Frank below.

The FDICIA has two important components that complement and support each other. First, Prompt Corrective Action (PCA) procedures prior to insolvency have the purpose of reducing the likelihood of insolvency as well as of increasing the preparedness for implementing insolvency procedures if necessary. Second, there are legally mandated rules for declaring insolvency and for procedures for dealing

---

[16]   Eisenbeis and Kaufman (2007) provide a summary of the US approach. See also US Shadow Financial Regulatory Committee, Statement 160, (2000).

[17]   Insolvency procedures for banks became separate from general bankruptcy law with the Banking Act of 1864. See Fitzpatrick IV et al. (2012).

with the insolvent bank and its stake-holders. These rules address several problems discussed above. In particular, the rules recognize the need for speed, that groups of creditors must be at risk, that the risk of contagion as a result of the insolvency must be low and that predictability of procedures reduces uncertainty about consequences of various action and strengthen incentives to take action to avert insolvency.

There are three characteristics of the US framework that stand out; the first is 'promptness' of all actions by the FDIC. The second is the specification of triggers for some action prior to insolvency (PCA). The third characteristic is that actions by the FDIC are legally mandated although exceptions became important during the sub-prime crisis. These characteristics contribute to early intervention, predictability for stakeholders and to reduced incentives for 'runs' on a bank in distress. PCA procedures will be described before turning to insolvency procedures.

6.1.1.   PCA: Prompt Corrective Action

The PCA procedures specified in the FDICIA represents a form of 'structured early intervention' with the purpose of reducing the likelihood that a bank approaching distress will actually fail and potentially become a systemic problem. The procedures also restore the buffer role of capital, since PCA allows capital to fall below the Basel based regulatory minimum but increasingly harsh constraints on activities are imposed on the banks at specific trigger capital ratios. The constraints impose predictable costs on banks' shareholders and management. In the words of Eisenbeis and Kaufman (2007), the PCA procedures serve as 'speed bumps' slowing down a bank's deterioration and forcing the FDIC to become involved well before insolvency occurs.

The sanctions described in Appendix 1 include change in senior management, reduction in dividends, restriction on acquisitions and adoption of capital restoration plans. If the bank is a subsidiary of a financial holding company, the parent loses its status as holding company relative to the bank subsidiary. These sanctions are imposed at specific trigger capital ratios that define zones of capitalization. The first trigger at a 10 percent capital ratio moves the bank from the well-capitalized zone to the adequately capitalized zone. The last trigger at two percent moves the bank into the 'critically under-capitalized' zone. In this zone the FDIC becomes conservator or receiver. Effectively, the bank is considered insolvent and the insolvency procedures described below apply.

Another feature of the PCA-procedures is that the trigger points are defined in terms of three different capital ratios. Two ratios are based on the Basel rules' definitions of risk-based Tier 1 and Tier 2 capital. The third ratio is a simple leverage ratio defined as book value of tangible equity relative to total on-balance sheet assets. Each capital ratio is binding meaning that each ratio triggers inter-

vention even if the trigger ratio has not been reached in terms of the other definitions. Appendix 1 shows the trigger ratios defining zones of capitalization and
required actions by the FDIC and the bank. It can be noted that the effectiveness
of the PCA rules have been questioned after the financial crisis on the grounds
that market value losses far exceeded the book value losses triggering PCA intervention.

6.1.2. US insolvency procedures

The FDICIA specifies a bank-closure rule that is triggered when a bank becomes
'critically under-capitalized' at a leverage ratio of two percent. Within 90 days the
bank must be declared legally insolvent, closed by the appropriate federal or state
authorities and placed in receivership or conservatorship. The bank charter is
revoked.

The reason for the two percent rules is that it provides a margin for a discrepancy
between the market value and the book value of assets, and errors in valuation.
Thereby the closure rule increases the likelihood that only shareholders will face
losses. The risk of runs by creditors is reduced by this margin. In general capital
turns out to be less than the book value. In fact, the market value of equity has
on average been negative at the time banks have been legally closed according to
Wall and Eisenbeis (2002).

After the closing of the bank (Step 1) the following steps are mandated:

Step 2: Prompt payment of insured deposits even if the bank is not
promptly reopened in Step 4 below.

Step 3: Prompt estimation and allocation of credit losses.

Step 4: Prompt reopening of large banks

Step 5: Prompt re-privatization and recapitalization

In step 1, depositors obtain immediate access to the insured parts of their deposits. Other creditors obtain access to their claims depending on their priority and
the estimated value of credit losses. The PCA procedures preceding insolvency
simplifies the important task for the FDIC to make a conservative estimate of
asset values in Step 3. Based on loss-estimates, pro-rata losses (haircuts) are allocated to claimants in order of legal priority. The FDIC stands in the shoes of
insured depositors. After making these depositors whole, the FDIC shares in the
losses with uninsured claimants.

The FDIC is required to manage the insolvency in order to achieve 'the least losses
to the deposit insurance fund.'

The legal closure of a bank need not imply physical closure in Step 4. In order to
avoid liquidity losses for a bank's creditors, the FDIC can sell the insolvent bank,

have another bank assume the claims on it or open a 'bridge bank' the day after the legal closure. This bridge bank would assume most or all of the assets of the failed bank at market value. The bridge bank provides time to find a buyer or to wind down the operations. Thus, 'fire sales' of the bank's assets can be avoided. In general, all actions should be based on the objective of minimizing losses to the deposit insurance fund. This objective implies that the conservator or receiver should aim to maximize the value of the assets and, thereby, take into consideration, for example, lack of liquidity and avoidance of 'fire sales'.

Uninsured depositors and other creditors do not receive payments immediately but 'receivership certificates'. They are paid in order of their legal priority when assets of the bank are sold. However, the FDIC has the authority to make advance payments on the basis of estimated recovery amounts in order to avoid liquidity contagion to former counterparties. In the case when a bridge bank is set up, the estimated recovery value can be transferred to the bridge bank enabling it to make payments to uninsured depositors. Borrowers with credit lines also maintain access to these lines in the bridge bank.

Estimates of the recovery value of funds advanced tend to be on the conservative side because the FDIC must absorb the loss of overestimates. If the recovery values have been underestimated the FDIC makes additional payments when assets are sold. The FDIC in its capacity as receiver can borrow the necessary funds to make advance payments in its corporate capacity with access to the FDIC's accumulated fund.

In the words of Eisenbeis and Kaufman, "the use of bridge banks... should eliminate much of the fear of bank failures. It should permit efficient resolution of large banks without strong negative reactions by the affected depositors and having to invoke the idea that some banks are 'too big to fail'." Clearly, this statement seems overly optimistic in the hindsight of the financial crisis,

As noted there is a legal requirement that insolvencies should be resolved at least cost to the FDIC. If asset values can be expected to fall in value during receivership, this requirement encourages rapid sales of assets. On the other hand, if low values depend on lack of liquidity in asset markets, the rule encourages the receiver to hold the assets until liquidity is restored.

In order to avoid the dangers of political influences and forbearance on bank closure decisions a bridge bank is specified in law to exist for a maximum of two years with the possibility of three one year extensions. In Step 5, the whole or part of the bank should be sold to the private sector within this time frame unless all assets have been sold already. The sale must result in a bank that is adequately capitalized at a minimum.

There is an exception to the FDICIA insolvency procedures when their implementation is likely to have serious systemic consequences. This 'systemic risk exception' leaves room for unequal treatment of creditors of banks considered 'too big to fail' by the Treasury Department, the Federal Reserve and the FDIC relative to creditors of small and mid-sized banks.

In 2009 the FDIC managed the closure of more than 100 small and medium sized (by US standards) banks but the government focused on the recapitalization of the very large international banks like Citibank and Bank of America. Thus, the FDICIA procedures have not been tested on a very large bank, most likely out of fear that the banks are too large, complex and systemically important to resolve under the procedures at a time when the capacity of the system is already strained.

The "Dodd Frank Wall Street Reform and Consumer Protection Act" that passed through the US Congress in 2010 addresses in Title II the 'too big to fail' issue by giving 'Orderly Liquidation Authority' to the FDIC for financial institutions that pose a risk to systemic stability. Through this authority non-bank financial institutions can be placed under FDIC receivership rather than being treated under general bankruptcy law under some circumstances[18]. The Act has the specific objective to prevent the use of tax-payers' funds to ensure the survival of systemically important bank and non-bank financial institutions. The FDIC can borrow temporarily from the Treasury to cover costs during receivership but the funds must be repaid from sales of unencumbered assets.

The credibility of the Act is yet to be tested. Two thirds of the members of the Board of Governors of the Federal Reserve System and two thirds of the board of the FDIC must recommend receivership to the Secretary of the Treasury, who, in consultation with the president, must decide whether criteria with respect to benefits of receivership are met. The alternative for non-bank financial institutions is general bankruptcy law.

The Dodd-Frank Act also introduces a requirement for Recovery and Resolution Plans (Living Wills) for Bank Holding Companies and for non-bank financial companies with assets greater than $50 billion. These companies are required to submit periodic reports regarding plans for rapid and orderly resolution under the bankruptcy code in the event of distress or failure. The living will requirement is intended to help regulators develop a comprehensive and coordinated resolution strategy for complex financial institutions.

---

[18]   See Fitzpatrick IV and Thomson (2011).

6.2.   The New Zealand approach

The general approach of New Zealand to banking regulation and supervision has been reliance on market discipline to a greater extent and more explicitly than any other country. The approach to regulation implemented in 1996 had the objective of being less prescriptive and less reliant on monitoring of individual financial institutions by supervisors. The regulation focused on disclosure of risk related information. The disclosure rules were intended to strengthen the ability of depositors and other creditors to evaluate the risk associated with lending to a bank. The financial crisis has led to a some re-evaluation of this approach.

Before the financial crisis New Zealand did not have a deposit insurance system. However, deposit guarantees were introduced during the financial crisis in 2008 and creditors of failing non-bank finance companies were fully covered by the government without waiting for the insolvency process to work itself out. Reforms implemented in 2011 signal an intent to return to a non-deposit insurance system while strengthening the resolution process in order to reduce the implicit insurance that may have been created by actions during the crisis (see Australia-New Zealand Shadow Financial Regulatory Committee, 2011).

The New Zealand procedure for bank insolvency is known as Open Bank Resolution (OBR). An insolvent bank or one likely to become insolvent can be placed under statutory management and continue to operate while decisions are made with respect to the final allocation of losses and future ownership. The Reserve Bank of New Zealand has the power to recommend to the Minister of Finance to appoint a statutory manager for a bank. The Statutory Manager is comparable to a Receiver in the US system.

Statutory management is considered an option of last resort. It requires systemic risk failure that allows for exception to standard corporate liquidation procedures. Alternative no-bail-out solutions like a merger with another bank should be unavailable.

When OBR is applied there is an immediate freeze on rights and claims against the bank. Restrictions on commercial activities are imposed. The Statutory Manager can sell assets and negotiate hair cuts on creditors' claims.

As in the US there is an emphasis on promptness in the resolution process. The bank should be re-opened as a bridge bank within a day. At this time haircuts on liabilities including deposits must be specified based on the Statutory Manager's initial estimates of the shortfall in the bank's capital position. Access to their remaining funds would be supported via a government guarantee.

Before the financial crisis there were no legally mandated procedures and principles for applying haircuts as in the US. Experiments have been conducted on procedures for making decisions with respect to haircuts and for making funds available quickly. These procedures for what is called 'Bank Creditor Recapitalization' are part of the 2011-revisions of the regulatory and legal framework for the financial sector in New Zealand.

One specific study of resolution procedures for New Zealand is reported on in Harrison, Anderson and Twaddle (2007). The study puts particular weight on 'pre-positioning' meaning that specific legal, operational and financial arrangements must be in place in order for resolution of a failed bank to be effective and prompt. The pre-positioning refers to the capability to implement procedures that look very much like the US FDICIA procedures described above. The following elements of pre-positioning are discussed:

1. closure of insolvent bank;
2. reserve a portion of creditors' claims to meet potential losses (haircuts);
3. next day release of remaining (non-frozen) claims in open bank under statutory management while the haircuts remain frozen;
4. government guarantee of non-frozen claims.

The pre-positioning involves the same elements as the formation of bridge bank in the US case. Legal capacity and legal powers must be clear, the operational capability must be in place even for a large complex bank and technological arrangements need to be worked out. Restrictions on out-sourcing of important functions of subsidiaries are intended to maintain technological and operational capabilities in New Zealand.

The current procedures for 'Bank Creditor Recapitalization' in New Zealand are similar to the US procedures but there is a stronger emphasis on pre-positioning in the sense that legal, operational and financial capability must be in place at the time insolvency occurs. 'Living wills' performs a similar role in the US. The problem of having the administrative capability to quickly implement the necessary steps in 'Bank Creditor Recapitalization' may be larger in a small country with relatively few banks and fewer bank failures than in the US with thousands of banks and management of failures almost routine. The structured early intervention (PCA) procedures in the US also contribute to the readiness for dealing with an insolvent bank.

The Australia-New Zealand Shadow Financial Regulatory Committee (2011) expresses some skepticism with respect to the practical value of the 'Bank Recapitalization Procedures'. The effectiveness of pre-positioning has not been tried and the capability to divide deposits into frozen and unfrozen parts within the day has never been implemented. If pre-positioning cannot be made credible implicit insurance may still exist and, thereby, the moral hazard problem requires attention.

An important characteristic of the New Zealand banking system is that it is relatively concentrated and dominated by subsidiaries of Australian banks. The foreign ownership creates specific problems from the point of view of crisis management since integrated international banks may be able to shift assets and risk among subsidiaries in different jurisdictions. For this reason, New Zealand subsidiaries are required to be able to operate on a stand alone basis within a day after Open Bank Resolution is initiated. One tool to achieve this objective is restrictions on outsourcing important functions to, for example, the foreign parent bank. Thereby, foreign controlled bank subsidiaries in New Zealand cannot remain as functionally integrated with the home country bank as is common elsewhere.

The reforms in 2011 indicate a shift in the approach to regulation and supervision in New Zealand. The Reserve Bank of New Zealand has assumed prudential responsibility for non bank finance and insurance companies. Therefore, the Open Bank Resolution can be applied on non-banks as well as banks. There is also a shift away from reliance on market discipline through disclosure towards private reporting of risk related information to the supervisor. In accordance with this shift supervision has become more intrusive and it covers the whole financial sector. The commitment to non-insurance of creditors including depositors remains, however. The experiences during the crisis with failing non-bank finance companies have shown that the non-insurance is credible only if the resolution procedures have a high degree of credibility. The increased emphasis on preparedness for prompt recapitalization within Open Bank Resolution can be seen in this light.

6.3. The UK Approach

Before 2009 there was no *lex specialis* for bank insolvency in the UK. The insolvency legislation for banks was the same as the legislation for non-financial corporation. The UK has special relatively quick administrative procedures for corporate insolvency which prior to the crisis were considered suitable for banks. Nevertheless, the British government felt compelled to intervene directly to rescue banks facing insolvency during the financial crisis.

A Special Resolution Regime (SRR) for banks was part of the Banking Act of 2009[19]. The SRR is part of a description of responsibilities and actions in times of banking crisis for the Treasury, the Financial Supervisory Authority (FSA) and the Bank of England (BOE). The FSA was once again made a part of the BOE with responsibility for supervision of individual banks while the Financial Policy Committee within the BOE has responsibility for macroprudential regulation.

---

[19] The description of the Special Resolution Regime is based on Avgouleas (2009).

The Act specifies four ways of dealing with a bank in distress: liquidity support, full insurance of deposits, public rescue and a special bankruptcy regime, the SRR. The objective of the SRR is to reduce the need to use the first three ways of dealing with distressed banks on the grounds that expectations that they will be used implies implicit protection of banks' creditors.

The SRR incorporates three stabilization options, special bank insolvency procedures (*lex specialis*) and a special bank administrative procedures. The stabilization options are:
(i)   transfer to private sector purchase;
(ii)   transfer of assets, rights and liabilities to a bridge bank owned by the BOE;
(iii)   temporary public ownership by the Treasury.

The FSA decides whether to apply SRR while the BOE decides which tool to use. Since the FSA lies within the BOE there is a substantial concentration of powers to the BOE.

The decision to apply the SRR requires that the bank is facing imminent failure no matter what. The private sector purchase, (i), and the creation of a bridge bank, (ii), depend on conditions with respect to stability, the public interest and protection of depositors. If public funds are put at risk as in a bridge bank the Treasury must be involved as well. All three stabilization options imply 'succession' and 'continuity' of property and legal rights.

If the stabilization options are unworkable the Special Bank Insolvency Regime comes into play. A court appoints a liquidator based on an application from the BOE. Eligible depositors under the deposit insurance scheme will have their accounts transferred before winding up procedures are initiated. The transfer of insured depositors' funds implies that public funds may be at risk if there are insufficient funds available in the deposit insurance fund.

The objective of the liquidation process is to achieve the best possible results for the creditors.

The third available tool under the SRR is the Special Administrative Procedure. This procedure is used when a part of the bank is sold off to a commercial buyer or to a bridge bank. A court rules on the Special Administration when a part of the bank is sold off and the residual of the bank is unable to pay its debt. The residual is then wound up as in the Special Bank Insolvency Regime.

The Banking Act of 2009 has been complemented in the Financial Services Act of 2010 with a requirement for Recovery and Resolution plans (Living Wills) as in the USA.

The SRR in the Banking Act applies to Commercial Banks but not to non-bank financial firms. The Vickers Report (UK Banking Commission, 2011) requires universal banks to 'ring-fence' commercial banking activities relative to investment banking activities. The SRR applies to the commercial banking activities but not to investment banking activities. The intent is to subject the latter activities to stronger market discipline while their need for special intervention to avoid contagion is less than for commercial banking activity. Market discipline should be present for commercial banking activities as well as a result of the possibility that creditors risk losses in the SRR procedures.

It can be noted that the UK regime explicitly limits the SRR to commercial banking activities while both the US and new Zealand have expanded their bank insolvency regimes to other activities than conventional commercial banking. We return to this coverage issue in the next section.

As noted above the UK bank insolvency regime consists of a menu of alternative approaches. The BOE stands at the center as the main authority deciding what to choose from this menu. Although trigger conditions for certain actions are included in the Banking Act, these conditions appear to be formulated in fairly general terms. Thus, the law offers substantial arbitrary power to the BOE while the emphasis in the USA before and after the crisis has been to mandate actions by the FDIC at specific trigger capital ratios. Thus, one can ask whether banks' creditors are credibly at risk in a severe crisis or if a bank is considered 'too big to fail.'

The credibility of the UK regime can be enhanced by a 'Code of Practice' that should be issued by the Government. Secondary legislation with respect to transfer of property such as rules for set-off and netting, secured liabilities, structured finance, and rights of counter parties can also contribute to the credibility of the SRR in the UK.

An additional credibility enhancing effect can potentially be obtained if the 'Living Will' requirement contributes to simpler and more transparent financial organizations. This issue will be discussed further below as an information issue.

6.4. Other countries

The US, New Zealand and the UK are not the only countries that have implemented special procedures for dealing with banks facing or approaching insolvency. The procedures in these countries are relatively elaborate and specific and, therefore, they can be considered 'model countries' for others that work on developments of special legislation for banks in distress. A few other countries with such legislation can be mentioned. Among these countries, Denmark can be emphasized as an additional 'model country' with a novel approach with relatively high credibility.

Denmark has implemented a resolution scheme for winding-up banks after September 30, 2010 in an amendment to the Act on Financial Stability[20]. At the same time a general guarantee scheme for banks expired. The key feature of the amendment is the existence of a permanent body, the Financial Stability Company, with the expertise and ability to manage the assets of a failed bank within a bridge bank, and to wind down this bank while allocating losses to non-insured creditors. A distressed bank's assets can be taken over by the Company if the bank does not satisfy regulatory capital requirements within a deadline set by the Financial Supervisory Authority. The bank is given the choice between going through general bankruptcy procedures as a corporation or being taken over by the Financial Stability Company.

The assets taken over by the Company in a new subsidiary bank are valued at market prices or, if there is no market price, at a "realization value" such that additional losses are unlikely to occur. As payment for the assets, a share of the unsubordinated liabilities is transferred to the new bank. The share is proportional to the total value of the unsubordinated liabilities relative to the realization value of the assets. Guaranteed deposits are covered by the Guarantee Fund for Depositors and Investors. The final realization value of the assets can be higher or lower than originally estimated. If they turn out to be lower, a Winding Up Fund takes the loss. This fund has been set up and ring-fenced within the Danish Guarantee Fund for Depositors and Investors. It is funded by the members of the fund, i.e. the banks in particular.

The evidence that the Danish approach to bank insolvency has lead to a credible reduction in implicit state support for banks' creditors is that the implementation of the new rules has led to an increase in funding costs and an increased premium on credit default swaps for Danish banks[21]."

A Swiss Commission of Experts (2010) has proposed reforms for *Switzerland* to reduce the problems caused by banks considered 'too big to fail.' This issue is particularly relevant for Switzerland with its two very large international universal banks. The proposals include capital requirements above those specified by the Basel Committee, liquidity and risk diversification requirements. The capital requirements include Contingent Convertible Debt (CoCos). Such debt converts to equity under specific conditions with respect to systemic conditions and bank's capital ratios.

The Swiss reforms also include procedures for allowing systemically important functions to continue in the event of a bank's insolvency and 'living wills' in the form of emergency plans for each large bank.

---

[20]   Ministry of Economic and Business Affairs, Denmark (2010).
[21]   For example, on February 20, 2012 the spread on interbank loans to the Danske Bank relative to Euribor was 7.05 basis points.

Germany implemented an 'Act for Restructuring of Credit Institutions' in January 2011. The act envisions a two step procedure beginning with measures to limit a bank's risk-taking before it reaches insolvency. The power to request such measures lies with the Bank Supervisory Authority (BaFin). The steps to limit banks' risk-taking can be compared to Prompt Corrective Action procedures although actions are mot legally mandated and there is not a series of triggers as in the US. Corporate Insolvency law still applies.

The most common approach to reform of bank resolution procedures in the wake of the crisis has been to designate a Resolution Authority with responsibility to manage distress in large banks and in the banking system. The Resolution Authority is given power to intervene in various ways to resolve a crisis. The Authority is given substantial arbitrary powers to intervene as it sees fit under the circumstances.

Sweden, as an example, has designated the National Debt Office (Riksgäldskontoret) as the resolution authority[22]. The authority has the right to use guarantees, capital injection, state takeover under certain conditions, and 'other manners' as resolution tools. An 'orderly resolution' can also be handled by the authority. In case of nationalization shares must be valued as if the company had not received state aid.

The tool box available for the Resolution Authority is large but there are few mandated procedures and, therefore, little predictability. Similarly, the 'orderly resolution' does not follow a legally mandated procedure.

In the specific Swedish case the funding of resolution is to be covered by a 'Stability Fund' once the fund, financed by a fee on banks, has reached sufficient size. The existence of such a fund may have the consequence that it increases the probability that the Resolution Authority chooses to bail out a large bank in a systemic crisis when speed of action is critical. Thus, the Stability Fund may contribute to implicit insurance of creditors of 'too big to fail' banks.

Not only relatively wealthy industrialized countries have developed insolvency procedures for banks. *Brazil* actually implemented a Bank Insolvency Act as early as in the mid 1960s (Sester, 2011) and it was applied during the 1970s crisis. In the mid 1990s the act was developed further as 'Programme to stimulate the Restructuring and Strengthening of the Financial System' (PROER). In 2005 a new Insolvency Law was implemented and further developed in 2009. The Law is divided into two parts covering intervention measures prior to insolvency and resolution measures.

---

[22]   October 2008, the Government Support to Credit Institutions Act (2008:814, 'Support Act').

Resolution is divided into three phases; special administration phase (90 days), intervention phase, and insolvency phase. This last phase is governed by a mix of bank specific insolvency procedures and procedures from general Brazilian Insolvency law. (See Sester, 2011)

There is also work within the *European Union* to develop a common framework for bank insolvency; in particular for large cross-border bank. The existing 'Cross-border Bank Insolvency Directive' (2001/24/EG) is limited in scope and applies only to cross-border banks with foreign branches. Insolvency of banks incorporated in member states is governed by national laws. There is a legislative process ongoing in the EU based on the view that full harmonization is needed to resolve cross-border banks. We return to this issue below.

7. KEY ISSUES FOR BANK INSOLVENCY LEGISLATION

In this section key issues that need to be addressed either in legislation for resolution of distressed banks or in complementary regulation are discussed briefly based on the approaches taken in the countries covered in the previous section. The issues discussed are *the contagion issue, the valuation issue, the predictability issue, the information issue, the coverage issue, the funding issue and the cross-border issue.*

7.1. The contagion issue

Much of the implicit protection of banks' creditors is based on authorities' fears of contagion through the financial system as a consequence of a large bank's or a number of banks' distress. Contagion creating systemic risk occurs through runs, domino effects through payment and settlement systems, price effects of fire sales and liquidity effects in securities markets.

Minimization of the risk of runs prior to insolvency is achieved primarily by means of the prompt re-opening of a 'bridge bank' after the declaration of insolvency and predictability of limited losses for uninsured creditors. The bridge bank makes funds available to insured depositors and funds minus haircuts available to non-insured claimants.

Many observers argue that the more serious systemic effects of a large bank's distress occur as a result of fire-sales of assets which may create a vicious circle of price declines, the need for additional sales in other banks leading to further price declines and so on. Liquidity in markets for important assets may also fall or disappear when banks are compelled to hoard liquidity and there is uncertainty about the solvency of many banks.

The price contagion is bound to occur well before a bank or banks becomes insolvent and made worse by rigid capital requirements. Procedures for Structured Early Intervention or Prompt Corrective Action in the US terminology make it possible to enhance the buffer role of capital. Thereby the need for fire sales is reduced. Outside the US there seems to be strong reluctance to include Structured Early Intervention in capital regulation. The prompt opening of a bridge bank after insolvency also contributes to a reduction in the supply of assets relative to a situation when a bank must be closed and assets liquidated.

Forbearance with a distressed bank may very well be the worst policy from the point of view of price and liquidity effects since the distress is not alleviated and, therefore, the bank must continue to economize on capital and hoard liquidity. Keeping so-called "Zombie banks" in operation will contribute to and increase the duration of price and liquidity effects as long as there is uncertainty about the time it will take to restore bank capital to a healthy level. Legally mandated and prompt procedures for both Structured Early Intervention and the closing of banks and allocation of losses increase predictability and transparency. Thereby, the liquidity problem caused by uncertainty about a bank's solvency is reduced.

The US procedures mandate that a bank must be closed when the capital ratio falls below two percent. Many observers in Europe argue that corporate law would not allow the closure of a bank before capital is exhausted. The advantage of having the trigger point for insolvency above zero is that it provides a margin increasing the likelihood that creditors will not have to face losses or only small losses. Thereby, the incentives for runs are weakened. Many observers in Europe argue that corporate law would not allow the closure of a bank before capital is exhausted. There are strong advantages to the US closure rule, however. If anything, an increase in the ratio that defines 'critically undercapitalized' could be considered.

Closing a bank while a bank has a positive value can be viewed as a violation of shareholders' rights. Uncertainty about actual values and the potential costs of waiting with closure are good reasons for making an exception to general corporate law and for requiring banks to incorporate this exception in their Charters.

7.2.   The valuation issue

The difficulty of valuing an insolvent firm's assets prevents rapid resolution. For corporations this issue is less serious than for financial institutions. The US insolvency regime does not solve this issue but reduces it by assessing conservative asset values to determine haircuts as a preliminary allocation of losses to creditors before the bridge bank opens. Greater conservatism implies greater losses, however. Therefore, the ability to make a quick, as well as realistic, valuation is important for the credibility of the insolvency regime with respect to large and complex banks in particular. This issue is discussed below as an *information issue.*

Mark-to-market accounting has no doubt contributed to the strength of the systemic risk caused by fire sales of assets and lack of liquidity in securities markets. On the other hand, mark-to-market accounting increases uncertainty about asset values. The risk-aware financial institution would therefore be induced to hold more capital under mark-to-market accounting than under historical value accounting. Similarly, the risk-aware financial institution would take into account that asset prices may fall as a result of low liquidity in specific markets. If liquidity risk is managed properly, the risk of contagion through the liquidity channel would be reduced as well. This reasoning presumes that there is strong risk awareness in financial institutions. In other words, strong market discipline and credible lack of forbearance by authorities are necessary requirements to induce financial institutions to hold extra capital and liquidity in response to volatility of market prices. The combination of marking to market valuation and moral hazard caused by explicit and implicit protection of creditors may very well be one of the primary causes of financial fragility.

Securities without liquid markets or no market pricing at all must be valued as well. 'Fair values' are then assessed by means of 'marking-to-similar assets' or 'marking-to-model.' These methods offer scope for arbitrariness and manipulation of asset values unless there are strong incentives for financial institutions to report valuation methods truthfully. It is possible that the healthy institutions have such incentives in order to access funding but experiences during the crisis indicate that many institutions have incentives to obfuscate. Thus, fair value accounting requires disclosure of valuation methods and assumptions. Incentives to manipulate the valuation may also be reduced by means of ex post personal liability of executives for misleading information disclosure.

7.3. The predictability issue

US procedures for early intervention as well as for legal closure and receivership are legally mandated. It would be legally indefensible for the FDIC to apply forbearance except when the 'escape clause' for systematically important banks applies. The legal mandate increases the predictability of actions and procedures for allocation of losses by reducing the discretionary power of the FDIC, the receiver and the bridge bank. Such predictability enhances market discipline by reducing the likelihood of implicit protection.

There are costs, as well, associated with a legal mandate for authorities to intervene at specific trigger-points with specific measures. In a particular situation, the 'first best' regulatory intervention may very well be different from the legally mandated intervention. However, the ability to use discretion tends to increase the so called time inconsistency problem and undermine credibility of stated policies.

The New Zealand and the UK regimes described in the previous section allow greater discretion than the US regime by making a menu of alternative distress resolution procedures available to policy and regulatory authorities. The closure of a bank and the setting up of a bridge bank is one alternative that can be used when the authorities consider it most appropriate. Discretion is a reality in the US as well as the recent crisis demonstrated. The FDICIA has an escape clause that allows the Fed, the Treasury and the FDIC to intervene by other measures than closure of systemically important banks. It is not yet clear how predictable the Orderly Liquidation Authority for large financial institutions under the Dodd-Frank Act will be. There are reasons to be skeptical since the ultimate judgment lies with the US Treasury in consultation with the president.

Denmark seems to have achieved a degree of credibility with respect to the application of insolvency procedures even for large banks as noted above. The setting up of a separate, permanent Financial Stability Company may have contributed to the credibility of the law.

There will always be room for a degree of discretion under any system since governments have the ultimate power to set rules and, thereby, to abandon rules. Maybe it is optimal to always have an escape under some unforeseeable circumstances but there is a trade-off between the credibility of the rule and the ability to act under very rare circumstances. One way of enhancing the credibility of a rule is to include a more diverse number of pre-specified actors in the decision mechanism for the escape clause.

Another factor affecting predictability is the objective of the legislated resolution procedures. In the US the explicit and mandated objective is to minimize the costs to the deposit insurance fund. Thereby, the receiver or the administrator of a failed bank must avoid destruction of value of ongoing operations as well as creditors' interest more generally. A loser objective is specified in the Basel Committee's (2012) recommendations for resolution regimes. This objective is 'the public interest' which leaves greater scope for actions that may protect specific interest groups.

7.4. The information issue

'Pre-positioning' in the New Zealand regime and Recovery and Resolution Plans (Living Wills) in the US and elsewhere increase the likelihood that relevant information as well as capability to evaluate assets will exist at the time a bank must be closed. The time between the closure of a bank and the opening of a bridge bank with haircuts deducted from creditors' claims is expected to be as short as one or two days in order to avoid severe repercussions from the closure of a large and complex bank. All assets and claims must be identified within complex structures with perhaps hundreds of subsidiaries and branches. The different entities may be functionally strongly integrated in spite of legal separation.

Harrison, Anderson and Twaddle (2007) emphasize the need for 'pre-positioning' meaning that specific legal, operational and financial arrangements must be in place in order for resolution of a failed bank to be effective in the sense that the risk of contagion is minimized. Decisions must be made rapidly with respect to the possible immediate sale of some entities and the immediate closure of some activities while other parts go into the bridge bank. The new bank must be functional quickly in order to obtain continued financing of activities.

The information required to implement haircuts is a complete mapping of assets and liabilities along with a preliminary valuation of all assets in order to assess the haircut that must be applied. The existence of Recovery and Resolution Plans (Living Wills) at the time of closure would contribute to the readiness to make rapid as well as realistic conservative valuation of the assets of the insolvent banks. As Avgouleas *et al.* (2011) point out such plans can also contribute to reorganization of financial institutions into less complex structures and thereby to increased transparency.

Recovery and Resolution Plans consist of two parts; a Recovery and a Resolution Plan. The first part sets out in detail what actions the bank would take to stay afloat in a distress situation by, for example, selling assets and/or business units. The Resolution Plan is a plan for unwinding the bank while saving critical functions. If the country has insolvency law for financial institutions, the latter part would have to be developed within the framework of the specific existing law.

One way to approach the requirement for financial institutions to develop Recovery and Resolution Plans is to incorporate the requirement in Structured Early Intervention (Prompt Corrective Action) procedures. If so the plan would have to be developed and updated when the capital ratio hits a certain trigger point. Thereby, crucial information for prompt resolution in insolvency such as counterparty and trading exposures, and opportunities for netting arrangements would be available at the time of closure.

Recovery and Resolution Plans (Living Wills) have become very popular among policy makers in the debate about financial reforms after the crisis. There is a risk that the reforms of resolution procedures will stop in many countries with such plans and the assignment of a Resolution authority without explicit legislation for insolvency procedures. Skepticism towards Living Wills has also been expressed by the IMF (2010), where it is pointed out that the feasibility of winding up strategies depend on the specific macro- and microeconomic conditions at the time of crisis. The German Bankers Association has also expressed fears that an existing plan may not work in a crisis with unforeseen circumstances[23].

The requirement that banks develop Recovery and Resolution Plans should not be seen as a substitute for explicit insolvency legislation. If such legislation exists, the plans would contribute to the preparedness for insolvency procedures by simplifying the information issue when insolvency occurs. The existence of specific insolvency legislation would guide the preparation of relevant information that otherwise can be prepared at some discretion by banking executives, who may have incentives to manipulate or obfuscate information. Incentives to make relevant information available at the time of closure within a specific insolvency regime can be enhanced by personal liability of executives.

Recovery and Resolution Plans are also discussed in connection with the cross-border issue below.

7.5.   The coverage issue

The recent financial crisis has demonstrated that a large number of non-bank financial institutions can obtain the same degree of maturity transformation as banks. In other words, banks are no longer special but systemic risk arises in non-bank financial institutions as well as in banks. If the insolvency law has the objective of enhancing market discipline and reducing systemic risk, it must be extended to cover all financial institutions with functionally similar activities.

The United States and New Zealand have recently extended the reach of special insolvency procedures to non-bank financial institutions while the UK has explicitly limited the special procedures to commercial banking in order to avoid that benefits of explicit deposit insurance and of implicit insurance of creditors extends to non-banking activities. One risk with the UK approach is that it over-emphasizes the 'specialness' of commercial banking. Thereby, it may strengthen the belief that large commercial banks will not be allowed to fail and that implicit insurance exists for banks' creditors.

The UK approach also risks strengthening the implicit insurance of creditors of non-banks unless market participants consider the application of general corporate law to non-bank financial institutions a credible option.

---

[23]   "Global Banks Forced to Write Living Wills", *The Financial Times*, October 4, 2012.

7.6.   The funding issue

The Dodd-Frank Act of 2010 has the specific objective to prevent the use of tax-payers' funds to ensure the survival of banks and systemically important non-bank financial institutions. Both the Dodd-Frank Act and the Danish resolution procedures make explicit how the costs of, for example, capitalization of a bridge bank are going to be covered without burdening the tax payers. Nevertheless, the tax payers are always going to be the ultimate guarantors of costs of implementing procedures.

The FDICIA legislation in the US specifies that the FDIC and ultimately US tax payers guarantee that creditors will not lose more than the haircut initially applied at the time of creation of a bridge bank. Even if haircuts are conservative there is a risk that losses may become larger than anticipated and that the bridge bank's capital is insufficient to cover all claims.

The funding of deposit insurance in the US and many other countries occurs through banks' payments of insurance premiums. These funds are reserved for depositors. If the fund is insufficient at the time of closure of a bank, either tax payers or depositors face losses. The US Congress has stepped in to provide additional funds to the FDIC in order to retain the credibility of the deposit insurance system. Iceland, on the other hand, was unable to fulfill its promises to depositors in foreign branches during the crisis.

The Icelandic case shows that the funding issue becomes particularly important for banks with very large foreign operations relative to the size of the home country. One consequence of this case is that it has increased the reluctance of supervisors and governments in host countries for foreign banks to rely on home country deposit insurance and home country supervision.

The existence of a pre-funded and substantial deposit insurance fund is particularly important for large banks in small countries but such a fund will generally contribute to lowering the risk of contagion through runs as well as to the credibility of closure rules.

Another aspect of the funding issue is so called bail-ins whereby private sector participants share in the burden. Bail-ins can be contractual as with issuance of Contingent Convertible bonds (CoCos) that convert into equity at a certain trigger capital ratio, or non-contractual if the resolution authority is given the power to, for example, convert bonds into equity.

7.7.   The cross-border issue

Cross-border issues have already been encountered in the discussions of information and coverage issues. The number of large banks with complex international structures has increased during the last few decades. Currently, US Bank Holding Companies own 6,000 entities engaged in a variety of activities entities outside the US. Regulatory and legal structures for crisis management have not been adapted along with the internationalization of banks. Approaches to crisis management and jurisdictional claims of national authorities over subsidiaries and branches may stand in conflict. Mechanisms to deal with distress are generally local in nature while financial operations of many large financial institutions are global. Some countries claim jurisdiction over the consolidated entity while others claim jurisdiction over formally incorporated entities in a country.

Cross-border banking can formally take place in subsidiaries or branches. In common terminology a subsidiary is a host country legal entity with its own capital as a buffer against losses and the subsidiary is subject to host country regulation, supervision and legislation. A host country branch, by the same terminology, is an integrated part of the home country bank subject to home country supervision, legislation and control. The branch does not have its own capital and it is subject to host country legislation and regulation only with respect to its conduct in the host country. The EU pushed these 'national' jurisdictional principles in the Banking Directive, allowing banks to operate across borders in branches under a 'Single License' within the EU subject to home country control and supervision. Crisis management procedures were not developed along with the Banking Directive; however, with the result that responsibility for resolution of a cross-border bank in crisis has remained ambiguous. This has contributed to the fact that most cross-border banking within the EU is formally conducted within subsidiaries.

The branch vs. subsidiary distinction in banking is not as clear as suggested above. Subsidiaries are often operated as more or less closely integrated risk-and liquidity planning entities. Branches are in many countries, including the US, required to have capital set aside for them. The functionally integrated cross-border bank can shift liquidity, assets and risk in various ways independent of legal organization. Asset losses can be shifted to one country and risk can be shifted to countries where capital requirement and supervision is weak. It can be argued that financial institutions have had an incentive to develop opaque organizational structures to increase their freedom to shift risk to tax payers in distress situations, and to increase the degree of implicit insurance for creditors as well as shareholders.

Work on the development of consistent principles for resolution of cross-border banks is ongoing in a number of international organization such as the IMF, the Financial Stability Board (FSB) within the G-20 group of countries, the Basel Committee and the EU[24]. Sester (2010) notes that "Progress has been made in many jurisdictions with the adoption of special administrative resolution regimes," but also that "consensus on general bank insolvency law at both the G-20 and the EU level remains out of reach." Thus, much work in international institutions focuses on truly systemic cross-border banks. The FSB notes the need for support tools for managing cross-border financial crisis, for information sharing about important aspects of structure of operations and inter-linkages among systematically important financial institutions (SIFIs) and for annual meetings to consider specific issues such as impediments to coordinated solutions. Banks should be capable of supplying information that may be required by authorities in a crisis and they should maintain contingency plans and procedures for use in a wind down situation. Practical barriers to efficient, internationally coordinated solutions should be removed and authorities should strive to find internationally coordinated solutions in times of crises. The FSB (2010b) recommends that all FSB jurisdictions have in place a policy framework to 'reduce the risks and externalities associated with' the domestic and global SIFIs in their jurisdictions.

All the above 'needs' are quite generally formulated. The FSB recommends that all countries should have a resolution framework so that all financial institutions can be safely and quickly resolved. SIFI resolution must be a viable option but there is little concrete about procedures for accomplishing these objectives.

The Basel Committee on Banking Supervision (2010a) also notes that national authorities should have appropriate tools to enable orderly resolution of all types of financial institutions including contingency plans for a period of distress that should facilitate winding down of institutions while preserving the system's functions. The European Commission (2010) as well as the IMF (2010b) supports the same principles as the FSB and the Basel Committee. In addition the EU aims to harmonize the EU regime for crisis prevention and bank recovery while the IMF aims to develop 'core coordination standards' and principles for burden sharing.

The private sector Institute for International Finance (IIF) puts substantial emphasis on reducing moral hazard. The IIF argues that resolution tools should be built on a contractual basis among legal entities. It objects to ring-fencing and develops specific features of insolvency regimes for cross-border banks. These features include specification of protected transactions and contracts, transfer of assets, liabilities and contracts, delay of termination clauses and powers to pre-

---

[24] See Basel Committee on Banking Supervision (2010, 2011), EU Commission (2010), Financial Stability Board (2010a, 2010b), Financial Stability Forum (2009), International Monetary Fund (2010b), Institute for International Finance (2011).

serve value. Critical functions should be isolated and transferred in the event of failure.

Although much of the reviewed work in international institutions is quite general there is convergence on the need for contingency plans for resolution, for information sharing among national supervisors about important aspects of banks' structures and inter-linkages, as well as for coordination to achieve burden-sharing in times of crises. There is now agreement that all G-20 countries should implement Recovery and Resolution Plans (Living Wills), including plans for coordination, information and burden sharing among national authorities. The FSB is expected to present a proposal for such plans in November 2012. Thus, Living Wills are expected to go far beyond information revelation to become an interactive process involving a financial institution and its supervisors in all countries potentially affected by a bank's failure.

Recovery and Resolution Plans (RRPs) have the potential to foster a common understanding on the structures of a group and their implications for crisis management and resolution as argued by Avgouleas *et al.* (2010). These authors also point out that RRPs may contribute to the simplification of international organization structures and, thereby, to transparency of cross-border SIFIs. However, the RRPs do not resolve fundamental sources of conflict with respect to burden sharing and potential jurisdictional conflicts among countries.

Another approach to reducing the potential for burden-sharing and jurisdictional conflicts would be to legislate that functional organizations must coincide with legal organizations. In other words, if a bank chooses to operate as a functionally integrated organization it must choose a branch organization while a subsidiary organization must consist of functionally and operationally separable entities[25]. New Zealand's approach to cross border banking is, as noted, to require subsidiaries of foreign banks to be able to quickly operationally separate themselves from the parent. Thereby, the likelihood that assets will 'disappear' from a bank approaching distress is reduced and domestic resolution procedures can be applied.

The point of making a clear distinction between subsidiaries and branches would be that host country insolvency law would apply to subsidiaries while home country law would apply to branches. Well-specified rule-based, home country insolvency procedures that prevent discrimination among claimants from different countries would enhance the acceptance in host countries of branches of foreign banks[26]. Without such 'mutual recognition' national supervisors would not be willing to respect and accept the legal structures as basis for resolution proce-

---

[25]   See Goldberg, Sweeney and Wihlborg (2005), Lastra and Wihlborg (2007) and Angkinand and Wihlborg (2012).

[26]   See Eisenbeis and Kaufman (2007) and Lastra and Wihlborg (2007) for discussion of this issue in an EU context.

dures. The EU Banking Directive envisions branch banking across borders within the EU under home country supervision but cross-border banking in subsidiaries dominates. The implementation of credible, rule-based insolvency law for banks in European countries can be viewed as a necessary requirement for the realization of the vision expressed in the Single Banking Act.

There are no doubt costs associated with functional structures coinciding with legal structures. For example, a cross-border bank would not be able to centralize liquidity planning within a subsidiary organization without having detailed contingencies for separation of funding sources. The same kind of separation requirement would most likely have to be one aspect of RRPs.

8. THE NEED FOR COMPLEMENTARY REFORMS OF FINANCIAL REGULATION

Effective procedures for dealing with banks in distress by means of structured early intervention and a *lex specialis* for insolvency of banks and similar financial institutions are no panacea offering optimal risk-taking incentives and the prospect of eternal financial stability. The procedures can strengthen market discipline on risk-taking and reduce the risk of systemic crisis but they must be viewed as one part on the financial architecture. Even if a *lex specialis* makes it possible for even large banks to fail it takes time for the procedures to gain credibility and implicit protection of large financial institutions to diminish. Cross-border banking implies that effective procedures must be implemented in many countries for credibility of lack of implicit protection to be achieved. Contagion through price and liquidity effects in securities markets remain a threat to the financial system.

Several aspects of the financial regulatory structure that would contribute to the effectiveness of resolution procedures without being part of insolvency legislation for financial institutions have been discussed above. Some important regulatory reforms that would enhance the effectiveness and credibility of insolvency procedures for systemically important financial institutions, in particular, are the following:

(i) structured Early Intervention at a series of trigger capital ratios (Prompt Corrective Action) well in advance of insolvency contributes to reducing the likelihood of insolvency as well as to clarification of costs of violating capital requirements. The trigger points can also be used to improve the readiness to deal with the financial institution in actual insolvency;

(ii) the information requirements associated with Recovery and Resolution Plans (Living Wills) can be linked to Structured Early Intervention to enable even a large and complex bank to be resolved quickly by means of sales of some functions while the remaining assets and liabilities after haircuts are transferred to a bridge bank;

(iii) higher capital requirements and potentially higher capital ratios triggering restrictions on activities and pre-positioning for resolution reduce the risk that large, sudden losses in a crisis make resolution authorities unprepared (European Shadow Financial Regulatory Committee, 2009a);

(iv) capital insurance as suggested by Kashyap, Rajan and Zingales (2008) enabling banks to increase equity contingent on large losses in asset value, and mandatory debt that converts to equity at a low capital ratio (Contingent Convertible debt) can be made part of Structured Early Intervention procedures. Such requirements would enhance the credibility of non-insurance of groups of creditors (US Shadow Financial Regulatory Committee, 2000, Flannery, 2005, and Östrup, 2007);

(v) greater flexibility in higher capital requirements would help restore the buffer role of capital and to reduce pro-cyclicality of capital requirements. The flexibility must be linked to specific conditions, however, to make costs of violations transparent;

(vi) clear and transparent valuation standards for assets based on marking-to-market valuation are necessary to implement both structured intervention and insolvency procedures. Clear standards for valuation of assets that are not traded are needed as well;

(vii) the resolution of cross-border banks according to bank insolvency law in either the home or the host country could be made possible with a minimum of burden-sharing and jurisdictional conflicts if foreign subsidiaries were required to be functionally and operationally separable as independent banks more or less overnight. Foreign owned subsidiaries in New Zealand operate under such a rule;

(viii) valuation and information rules can be made more effective by means of personal liability of bank executives;

(ix) capital requirements could take into account liquidity risk by linking capital requirements to the maturity mismatch and, thereby, discourage long term positions being financed with very short term financial instruments (Brunnermeier *et al.*, 2009);

(x) the central bank as a lender of last resort remains important but this function should not be used to subsidize financial institutions. Decision-making with fiscal implications should be the responsibility of fiscal authorities.

9. CONCLUSIONS AND ONGOING INTERNATIONAL WORK ON INSOLVENCY PROCEDURES.

Effective procedures for allocation of losses of banks in distress would allocate the losses to shareholders and creditors with a minimum risk of contagion and without serious disruption of the financial system. The lack of effective resolution procedures has been a source of substantial implicit protection of banks' creditors and, therefore, of excessive risk-taking. The competitive mechanism that serves to increase efficiency in other industries has not functioned well in banking where inefficient banks may be the first to obtain protection in a crisis. Large and complex banks considered either too big or too complex to fail have enjoyed an implicit subsidy.

The need for a *lex specialis* for resolution of insolvent banks and other financial institutions serving similar functions, and requirements for making resolution procedures effective have been discussed in this paper. Approaches to resolution procedures in a few 'model countries' were described following a review of the objectives of general insolvency law, and the special characteristics of banks and the financial system which provide the basis for the design of a *lex specialis*.

The issues that require attention in legislation for resolution procedures were identified as the contagion issue, the valuation issue, the predictability issue, the information issue, the coverage issue, the funding issue and the cross-border issue. Complementary reforms of the financial architecture that would enhance the effectiveness of legislation for resolution procedures were discussed as well.

The Basel Committee (2011) reviews the progress on resolution policies and frameworks up to mid 2011. The above issues are addressed with different degrees of emphasis by the Basel Committee. It recommends that each country should implement a Special Resolution Regime (SSR) that should enable the closure of even large banks. The characteristics of the recommended SSR are most like those contained in the UK approach reviewed in Section 6.

Although the Basel Committee refers to predictability of insolvency procedures, its major emphasis lies on 'Powers' of Resolution Authorities to close and resolve a bank by means of, for example, sales of critical functions and transfers of assets and liabilities to a bridge bank. As noted in the discussion of the predictability issue it may not be sufficient to enable resolution in a crisis unless the powers are accompanied by a 'Mandate' to apply the different alternative resolution methods under specific conditions. The predictability of the use of powers is reduced further by an objective defined only in terms of the 'public interest.'

A second emphasis of the Basel Committee lies on 'Powers' to implement early intervention to require risk mitigation, information disclosure and other actions.

Again the powers are not accompanied by a mandate and there is no specification of trigger capital ratios as in the US FDICIA procedures.

The country that has gone the farthest towards a mandate for application of structured early intervention as well as insolvency procedures is the United States. Even there an escape clause made it possible to bypass the mandate and bail-out systemically important banks during the crisis. There are attempts to make the escape clause more restrictive, however. At the same time, the Orderly Liquidation Authority for systemically important financial institutions in the Dodd-Frank Act does not include a mandate but leaves the trade-off between bail-out and orderly liquidation to regulatory and policy authorities. The approach taken by Denmark, including the formation of a permanent Financial Stability Company with responsibility for liquidation, may be a promising route to achieving predictability with respect to resolution of large banks.

Two issues that must be addressed in order to make it possible to apply resolution procedures on large financial institutions are the information issue and the cross-border issue. The Basel Committee reports only limited progress on the cross-border issue so far but there is greater progress on the information issue. This issue is addressed through Recovery and Resolution Procedures or 'Living Wills' as they are often called. Several countries are in the process of implementing Living Wills and the Financial Stability Board is expected to publish detailed recommendations in November 2012.

Recovery and Resolution Procedures prepare for resolution by providing detailed information about assets, liabilities and contractual arrangements well in advance, and by stating plans for recovery through sales of assets or entities as well as plans for resolution. These plans are to be worked out in cooperation with supervisors.

As noted by Avgouleas *et al.* (2010) Recovery and Resolution Procedures hold promise that a Resolution Authority or insolvency administrator will be 'pre-positioned' to deal promptly with an insolvent bank with knowledge of activities that must be sold or transferred to a bridge bank. The planning for recovery and resolution may also provide incentives for large banks, including cross-border banks, to simplify their organizational structures that often are designed to be opaque.

There is a risk that the reforms of resolution procedures will stop in many countries with Living Wills and the assignment of a powers to Resolution authority without explicit legislation for insolvency procedures. Living Wills should not be seen as a substitute for explicit insolvency legislation. The existence of a plan does not guarantee that it will work under unforeseen circumstances of a crisis. Explicit and specific insolvency legislation would guide the preparation of relevant information that otherwise can be prepared at some discretion by banking executives, who may have incentives to manipulate or obfuscate information.

The recent crisis has lead to a re-evaluation of the channels of contagion that may create systemic risk in the financial system. In particular, contagion through price changes on securities and liquidity in markets for securities have been emphasized by several economists while the more traditional contagion through payment and settlement systems have become less of a threat as a result of innovations in these systems. The emphasis on price and liquidity contagion has implications for the financial regulatory framework as a whole as well as for procedures for dealing with financial institutions in distress.

One implication of the new view of systemic risk is that special insolvency law may have to cover non-bank financial institutions as well as banks. A second implication is that flexibility in the required (higher) capital ratio can reduce the need for fire sales of assets. 'Structured early intervention' prior to insolvency along the lines of Prompt Corrective Action procedures is one way of achieving such flexibility while reducing the probability that a financial institution will reach the default point. Third, principles for valuation of assets must be transparent and clear since they affect points of intervention and insolvency.

Work on resolution procedures in Europe, in particular, put strong emphasis on a harmonized approach, which may be impossible to achieve. An alternative way to reduce the scope for jurisdictional and burden-sharing conflicts among national authorities would be to make the functional organizations of cross-border banks consistent with the legal organizations in subsidiaries or branches while retaining differences in resolution procedures. The responsibility of home and host country jurisdictions could thereby be clarified.

REFERENCES

ADRIAN, T. and SHIN, H.S. (2007), "Liquidity, Financial Cycles and Monetary Policy" in *Current Issues in Economics and Finance*, Federal Reserve Bank of New York, Vol. 14, No. 1.

ANGKINAND, A. and WIHLBORG, C. (2006), "Bank Insolvency Procedures as Foundation for Market Discipline" in G. CAPRIO, D. EVANOFF and G. KAUFMAN (eds.), *Cross-border Banking*, World Economic Publishers.

ANGKINAND, A. and WIHLBORG, C. (2012), "Cross-border Banking in Subsidiaries and Branches; Organization, Supervision and Resolution" in G. CAPRIO (ed.), *The Encyclopedia of Financial Globalization*, Forthcoming.

AVGOULEAS, E. (2009), "Banking Supervision and the Special Resolution Regime of the Banking Act 2009; the Unfinished Reform", *Capital Markets Law Journal*, March.

AVGOULEAS, E., GOODHART, C. and SCHOENMAKER, D. (2010), "Bank Resolution Plans as Catalyst for Action", *Journal of Financial Stability*, January.

AUSTRALIA-NEW ZEALAND SHADOW FINANCIAL REGULATORY COMMITTEE (2011), "The Global Financial Crisis and Financial Regulation In The Antipodes" in R. LITAN (ed.), *World in Crisis: Insights from Six Shadow Financial Regulatory Committees From Around the World*, Wharton Financial Institutions Center, U. of Pennsylvania, November.

BASEL COMMITTEE ON BANKING SUPERVISION (2010), *Report and Recommendations of the Cross-border Bank Resolution Group*, March, Basel.

BASEL COMMITTEE ON BANKING SUPERVISION (2011), *Resolution Policies and Frameworks Progress so far*, July 7, Basel.

BOLLARD, A. (2004). "Systemic Financial Crisis; Resolving Large Bank Insolvencies", *Reserve Bank of New Zealand Bulletin*, December, Vol. 67, No. 4.

BOLLARD, A. (2005), "Bank Regulation and Supervision in New Zealand; Recent and Ongoing Developments", *Reserve Bank of New Zealand Bulletin*, June, Vol. 68, 2

BOOT, A.W.A. (2006), *Supervisory Arrangements, LOLR and Crisis Management in a Single European Banking Market*, Conference Paper, Federal Reserve Bank of Chicago, October 5-6, 2006.

BRUNNERMEIER, M., CROCKET, A., GOODHART, C., HELLWIG, M., PERSAUD, A. and SHIN, H. S. (2009), "The Fundamental Principles of Financial Regulation", *Geneva Report on the World Economy*, 11, January 6.

BRUNNERMEIER, M. and PEDERSEN, L., "Market Liquidity and Funding Liquidity", *Review of Financial Studies* 2009.

CAMPBELL, A. (2003), "Issues in Cross-Border Bank Insolvency: The European Community Directive on the Reorganization and Winding Up of Credit Institutions" in *Current Developments in Monetary and Financial Law*, Vol. 3, Washington DC, International Monetary Fund, 2003.

COCHRANE, J. N. (2009), *The Financial Crisis and Policy*, Presentation at the Cato Institute, New York, November 5.

COCHRANE, J. and ZINGALES, L. (2009), "Lehman and the Financial Crisis", *The Wall Street Journal* November 15.

COHEN, W. (2008), "Why Wall Street has to Alter its Incentives", *Financial Times* March 17.

EISENBEIS, R. and KAUFMAN, G. (2007), "Cross-Border Banking: Challenges for Deposit Insurance and Financial Stability in the European Union" in H. BENINK, C. GOODHART and R.M. LASTRA (eds.), *Prompt Corrective Action and Cross-border Supervisory Issues in Europe*, FMG Special Paper 171, London Schoool of Economics.

EU COMMISSION (2010), *Communication on Crisis Management in the Financial Sector*, October.

EUROPEAN SHADOW FINANCIAL REGULATORY COMMITTEE (1998), *Resolving problem banks in Europe*, Statement No. 1, London.

EUROPEAN SHADOW FINANCIAL REGULATORY COMMITTEE (2009a), *The Financial Crisis and the Future of Financial Regulation*, Statement No. 28, London, January 19.

EUROPEAN SHADOW FINANCIAL REGULATORY COMMITTEE (2009b), *Letter to the G20*, Statement No. 30, Warsaw, September 21.

FEDERAL DEPOSIT INSURANCE CORPORATION IMPROVEMENT ACT (FDICIA) (1991).

FINANCIAL STABILITY BOARD (2010a), *Interim Report to G20 Leaders*, June.

FINANCIAL STABILITY BOARD (2010b), *Reducing the Moral Hazard Posed by Systematically Important Financial Institutions*, October.

FINANCIAL STABILITY FORUM (2009), *Principles for Cross-Border Cooperation on Crisis Management*, April 2, Basel.

FITZPATRICK IV, T. J. and J. B. THOMSON (2011), "An End to Too Big o Let Fail? The Dodd-Frank Act's Orderly Liquidation Authority," Economic Commentary, 1, Jan. 5, Federal Reserve Bank of Cleveland.

FITZPATRICK IV, T.J., M. K. MARKS and J.B. THOMSON (2012), "The History and Rationale for A Separate Bank Resolution Process," Economic Commentary, 1, Febr. 2, Federal Reserve Bank of Cleveland.

FLANNERY, M. (2005), "No pain, no gain? Effective Market Discipline via Reverse Convertible Debentures", Chapter 5 in H.S. SCOTT (ed.), *Capital Adequacy Beyond Basel: Banking, Securities and Insurance*, Oxford, Oxford University Press.

GOLDBERG, L., SWEENEY, R.J. and WIHLBORG, C. (2005), "Can Nordea show Europe the way?", *The Financial Regulator*, Vol. 10, No. 2, September.

GOODHART, C. (ed.) (2000), *Which Lender of Last Resort for Europe*, London, Central Banking Publications.

HARRISON, I., ANDERSON, S. and TWADDLE, J. (2007), "Pre-positioning for Effective Resolution of Bank Failures", *Journal of Financial Stability*, Vol. 13, No. 4, pp. 324-341.

HERRING, R. (2004), *International financial conglomerates; Implications for bank insolvency regimes*, Financial Institutions Center, The Wharton School, Working Paper.

HÜPKES, E. (2003), "Insolvency – Why a Special Regime for Banks" in *Current Developments in Monetary and Financial Law*, Vol. 3, Washington D.C., International Monetary Fund.

Huertas, T.F. (2007), "Dealing with Distress in Financial Conglomerates" in H. Benink, C. Goodhart and R.M. Lastra (eds.), *Prompt Corrective Action and Cross-border Supervisory Issues in Europe*, FMG Special Paper 171, London School of Economics.

Institute for International Finance (2011), *A Global Approach to Resolving Failing Financial Firms: An Industry Perspective*, May, Washington D.C.

International Monetary Fund (2010a), *IMF Contribution to EU Consultation on an EU Framework for Cross-border Crisis Management in the Banking sector*, January, Washington D.C.

International Monetary Fund (2010b), *Resolution of Cross-border banks – A proposed framework for enhanced coordination*, June 11, Washington D.C.

Kashyap, A.K., Rajan, R.G. and Stein, J.C. (2008), *Rethinking Capital Regulation*, Symposium on Maintaining Stability in a Changing Financial System, Federal Reserve Bank of Kansas City, August 21-23.

Krimminger, M. (2005), "Deposit Insurance and Bank Insolvency in a Changing World: Synergies and Challenges" in *Current Developments in Monetary and Financial Law*, Vol. 4, Washington D.C., International Monetary Fund

Lastra, R. (2006), *Legal Foundations of International Monetary Stability*, Oxford University Press.

Lastra, R. and Wihlborg, C. (2007), "Law and Economics of Crisis Resolution in Cross-border Banking" in H. Benink, C. Goodhart and R.M. Lastra (eds.), *Prompt Corrective Action and Cross-border Supervisory Issues in Europe*, FMG Special Paper 171, London Schoool of Economics.

Llewellyn, D. T. (2010), *A Framework for Crisis Prevention and Management: Where is Pillar 4?*, paper presented at Annual Colloquium of the Belgian Financial Forum, November 10, Working Paper, London, International Centre for Financial Regulation.

Mayes, D. (2004), "Who pays for Bank Insolvency", *Journal of International Money and Finance*, Vol. 23, pp. 515-551.

Mayes, D. and Liuksila, A. (eds.) (2004), *Who Pays for Bank Insolvency?*, Hampshire and New York, Palgrave, MacMillan.

Ministry of Economic and Business Affairs, Denmark (2010), *Danish Act on Financial Stability*, Act No. 721 of 25 June 2010, Copenhagen.

Östrup, F. (2007), *Finansielle kriser*, Copenhagen, CBS Press.

Schiffman, H. (1999), "Legal Measures to Manage Bank Insolvency" in R. Lastra and H. Schiffman (eds.), *Bank Failures and Bank Insolvency Law in Economies in Transition*, The Hague, Kluwer Law International.

SESTER, P. (2011), "Towards a Transnational Bank Restructuring Law? The attempt of the G20 to initiate and monitor regulatory responses to the 'too big to fail' problem", *European Company and Financial Law Review*, Vol. 7, Issue 4, pp. 512-549.

STATENS OFFENTLIGA UTREDNINGAR (2000), *Offentlig Administration av Banker*, Stockholm, SOU 2000:66.

SWISS COMMISSION OF EXPERTS (2010), *Final report of the Commission of Experts for limiting economic risk posed by large companies*, September 30.

UK Banking Commission (2011), *Interim Report Consultation on Reform Options*, April.

U.S. SHADOW FINANCIAL REGULATORY COMMITTEE (2000), *Reforming Bank Capital Regulation: A Proposal by the U.S. Shadow Financial Regulatory Committee*, Statement No. 160, Washington, DC, American Enterprise Institute.

WALL, L.D. and EISENBEIS, R.A. (2002), "Reforming Deposit Insurance and FDI-CIA?", *Economic Review*, Federal Reserve Bank of Atlanta, First Quarter, pp. 1-16.

WIHLBORG, C., GANGOPADHYAY, S. and HUSSAIN, Q. (2001), "Infrastructure requirements in the area of bankruptcy", *Brookings-Wharton Papers on Financial Services*.

Appendix 1. US Prompt Corrective Action (PCA) Trigger Capital Ratios and Provisions in different zones for capital ratios (Eisenbeis and Kaufman (2007)

Zone	Mandatory Provisions	Discretionary Provisions	Risk Based Capital Ratio (%); Total	Risk Based Capital Ratio (%); Tier 1	Leverage Ratio (%)
1. Well capitalized			>10	>6	>5
2. Adequately Capitalized	Brokered deposits only with FDIC approval		>8	>4	>4
3. Under-capitalized	Suspend dividends and mgmt fees; Require capital restoration plans; Restrict asset growth; Approval required for acquisitions, branching and new activities	Order recapitalization; Restrict inter-affiliate transactions, deposit interest rates, other activities	<8	<4	<4
4. Significantly Under-capitalized	Order re-capitalization; Restrict inter-affiliate transactions and deposit interest rates; pay of officers restricted	Conservatorship or receivership if bank fails to submit or implement plan to recapitalize pursuant to order: Zone 5 provisions if necessary to carry out PCA	<6	<3	<3
5. Critically Under-capitalized	Receivership or conservatorship within 90 days Receiver if still in zone after 4 quarters; Suspend payments on subordinated debt; Restrict other activities			<2	<2

SUERF – Société Universitaire Européenne de Recherches Financières

SUERF is incorporated in France as a non-profit-making Association. It was founded in 1963 as a European-wide forum with the aim of bringing together professionals from both the practitioner and academic sides of finance who have an interest in the working of financial markets, institutions and systems, and the conduct of monetary and regulatory policy. SUERF is a network association of central bankers, bankers and other practitioners in the financial sector, and academics with the purpose of analysing and understanding European financial markets, institutions and systems, and the conduct of regulation and monetary policy. It organises regular Colloquia, lectures and seminars and each year publishes several analytical studies in the form of *SUERF Studies*.

SUERF has its full-time permanent Executive Office and Secretariat located at the Austrian National Bank in Vienna. It is financed by annual corporate, personal and academic institution membership fees. Corporate membership currently includes major European financial institutions and Central Banks. SUERF is strongly supported by Central Banks in Europe and its membership comprises most of Europe's Central Banks (including the Bank for International Settlements and the European Central Bank), banks, other financial institutions and academics.

SUERF Studies

1997-2010

For details of SUERF Studies published prior to 2011 (Nos. 1 to 22 and 2003/1-2010/5) please consult the SUERF website at www.suerf.org.

2011

2011/1   *The Future of Banking in CESEE after the Financial Crisis*, edited by Attilla Csajbók and Ernest Gnan, Vienna 2011, ISBN 978-3-902109-56-9

2011/2   *Regulation and Banking after the Crisis*, edited by Frank Browne, David T. Llewellyn and Philip Molyneux, Vienna 2011, ISBN 978-3-902109-57-6

2011/3   *Monetary Policy after the Crisis*, edited by Ernest Gnan, Ryszard Kokoszczynski, Tomasz Łyziak and Robert McCauley, Vienna 2011, ISBN 978-3-902109-58-3

2011/4   *Divergence of Risk Indicators and the Conditions for Market Discipline in Banking*, Vienna 2011, ISBN 978-3-902109-59-0

2011/5   *Roles, Missions and Business Models of Public Financial Institutions in Europe*, Vienna 2011, ISBN 978-3-902109-60-6

2012

2012/1   *New Paradigms in Monetary Theory and Policy?*, edited by Morten Balling and David T. Llewellyn, Vienna 2012, ISBN 978-3-9021-0961-3

2012/2   *New Paradigms in Banking, Financial Markets and Regulations?*, edited by Morten Balling, Frank Lierman, Freddy Van den Spiegel, Rym Ayadi and David T. Llewellyn, Vienna 2012, ISBN 978-3-9021-62-0

2012/3   *Future Risks and Fragilities for Financial Stability*, edited by David T. Llewellyn and Richard Reid, Vienna 2012, ISBN 978-3-9021-0963-7

2012/4   *The ESRB at 1*, edited by Ernest Gnan, Stefan Gerlach and Jens Ulbrich, Vienna, 2012, ISBN 978-3-9021-0964-4